NIGHTWATCH

NIGHTWATCH

New & Selected Poems 1968–1996

PHOTO: SUSAN PERLY

Nightwatch

NEW & SELECTED POEMS 1968–1996

Dennis Lee

THE MODERN CANADIAN POETS SERIES

Canadian Cataloguing in Publication Data

Lee, Dennis, 1939 –
Nightwatch
(The Modern Canadian Poets)

ISBN 0-7710-5215-4
I. Title.   II. Series.
PS8523.E3N5 1996   C811'.54   C95-932955-2
PR9199.3.L44N5 1996

The publishers acknowledge the support of the Canada Council and the Ontario Arts Council for their publishing program. ¶ Printed and bound in Canada. ¶ The paper used in this book is acid-free.

McClelland & Stewart Inc.
The Canadian Publishers
481 University Ave.
Toronto, Ontario
M5G 2E9

1   2   3   4   5   00   99   98   97   96

Susan

CONTENTS

11   CIVIL ELEGIES (1968, 1972)

43   THE DEATH OF HAROLD LADOO (1976, 1979)

67   NOT ABSTRACT HARMONIES BUT (1972–1996)

69   *400: Coming Home*

71   *Recollection*

72   *High Park, by Grenadier Pond*

74   *Sibelius Park*

78   *Coming Back*

79   *Simple Songs*

81   *Spring Song*

83   *After Dinner Music*

85   *Not Abstract Harmonies But*

89   *You Too Lie Down*

90   *Coming Becomes You*

91   *East of the Moment*

92   *Oblivion River*

94   *Downward of Roses*

95   *The Gods*

101   RIFFS (1982, 1993)

167   NIGHTWATCH (1996)

169   *Nightwatch* (Dark house)

177   *Blue Psalm* (Keep low, my life)

178   *Something about a Train*

179   *Blue Psalm* (Hush hush, little wanderer)

181   *Nightwatch* (Back with the scotch)

187   *Cadence*

189   *Blue Psalm* (How late, my life)
190   *One More Morning*
192   *Blue Psalm* (When first we came to this land)
194   *Night Songs*
201   *Hunger*
203   *Heart Residence*

CIVIL ELEGIES

Man is by nature a political animal, and to know that citizenship is an impossibility is to be cut off from one of the highest forms of life.

GEORGE GRANT

Do not cling to the notion of emptiness:
Consider all things alike. My friend,
There is only one word that I know now,
And I do not know its name.

SARAHA

§

Toronto's New City Hall opened in 1965. Two curved white towers gave onto a great square; at the time, such a dramatic public space was new in Toronto.

1

Often I sit in the sun and brooding over the city, always
in airborne shapes among the pollution I hear them, returning;
pouring across the square
in fetid descent they darken the towers
and the wind-swept place of meeting, and whenever
the thick air clogs my breathing it teems with their presence.
Many were born in Canada, and living unlived lives they died
of course but died truncated, stunted, never at
home in native space and not yet
citizens of a human body of kind. And it is Canada
that specialized in this deprivation. Therefore the spectres arrive,
    congregating
in bitter droves, thick in the April sunlight,
accusing us and we are no different, though you would not expect
the furies assembled in hogtown and ring me round, invisible, demanding
what time of our lives we wait for till we shall start to be.
Until they come the wide square stretches out
serene, and singly by moments it takes us in, each one for now
a passionate civil man – until it
sends us back to the acres of gutted intentions,
back to the concrete debris, to parking scars and the four-square tiers
of squat and righteous lives. And here
once more, I watch the homing furies' arrival.

I sat one morning by the Moore, off to the west
ten yards, and saw though diffident my city nailed against the sky
in ordinary glory.
And dreamed a better past. A place, a making,

two towers, a teeming, a genesis, a city.
And the men and women performed their daily lives
by ancient measure, patricians in muddy York,
and made their compact together against the gangs of the new.
And as that crumpled before the shambling onset, again the
lives we had not lived in phalanx invisibly staining
the square and vistas, casting back I saw
regeneration twirl its blood and the rebels riding
riderless down Yonge Street, plain men much
goaded by privilege – our other origin, and cried,
"Mackenzie knows a word! Mackenzie
knows a meaning!" but it was not true. Eight-hundred-odd steely
     insurgents
turned tail at the cabbage patch when a couple of bullets fizzed
and the loyalists, scared skinny by the sound of their own gunfire,
gawked and bolted south to the fort like rabbits,
the rebels for their part bolting north to the pub: the first
spontaneous mutual retreat in the history of warfare.
Canadians, in flight.

Buildings oppress me, and the sky-concealing wires
bunch zigzag through the air. I know
the dead persist in
by-laws, roadways, porticos – the city I live in
is clogged with their presence; they
dawdle about in our lives and form a destiny, still
incomplete, still dead weight, still
demanding whether Canada will be.

But the mad bomber, Chartier of Major Street, Chartier
said it: that if a country has no living past to learn from,
neither is it a country, and promptly

blew himself to bits in the parliament john, leaving as civil testament
assorted chunks of prophet, twitching and
bobbing to rest in the flush.
And what can anyone do in this country, baffled and
making our penance for ancestors, what did they leave us? Indian-
     swindlers,
stewards of unclaimed earth and rootless what does it matter if they, our
forebears' flesh and bone were often
good men? Good men do not matter to history.
And what can we do here now, for at last we have no notion
what we might have come to be in America, alternative, and how make
     public
a presence which is not sold out utterly to the modern? utterly? to the
savage inflictions of what is for real, it pays off, it is only
accidentally less than human?

In the city I long for, green trees still
asphyxiate. The crowds emerge at five from jobs
that rankle and lag. Heavy developers
pay off aldermen still; the craft of neighbourhood,
its whichway streets and generations
anger the planners, they go on jamming maps
with asphalt panaceas; single men
still eke out evenings courting, in rooms, alone.
A man could spend a lifetime looking for
peace in that city. And the lives give way around him – marriages
founder, neighbourhoods sag – until
the emptiness comes down on him to stay.
But in the city I long for, the people complete
their origins. Among the tangle of
hydro, hydrants, second mortgages, amid
the itch for new debentures, greater expressways,

in sober alarm they jam their works of progress, asking where in truth
they come from and to whom they must belong.
And thus they clear a space in which
the full desires of those that begot them, great animating desires
that shrank and grew hectic as the land pre-empted their lives
might still take root, which eddy now and
drift in the square, being neither alive nor dead.
And the people accept a flawed inheritance
and they give it a place in their midst, forfeiting progress, forfeiting
dollars, forfeiting yankee visions of cities that in time it might grow
whole at last in their lives, they might
belong once more to their forebears, becoming their own men.

To be our own men! in dread to live
the land, our own harsh country, beloved, the prairie, the foothills –
and for me it is lake by rapids by stream-fed lake, threading
north through the terminal vistas of black spruce, in a
bitter, cherished land it is farm after
farm in the waste of the continental outcrop –
for me it is Shield but wherever terrain informs our lives and claims us;
and then, no longer haunted by
unlived presence, to live the cities:
to furnish, out of the traffic and smog and the shambles of dead
      precursors,
a civil habitation that is
human, and our own.

The spectres drift across the square in rows.
How empire permeates! And we sit down
in Nathan Phillips Square, among the sun,

as if our lives were real.
Headlines! high-rise! neon hieroglyphics!
And the towers' luminous sign, that not
one countryman has learned, that
men and women live that
they may make that
life worth dying. Living. Hey,
the dead ones! Gentlemen, generations of
acquiescent spectres gawk at the chrome
on American cars on Queen Street, gawk and slump and retreat.
And over the square where I sit, congregating above the Archer
they crowd in a dense baffled throng and the sun does not shine through.

2

Master and Lord, where
are you?
A man moves back and forth
between what must be done to save the world
and what will save his soul,
and neither is real. For many years
I could not speak your name, nor now but
even stilled at times by openings like
joy my whole life
aches, the streets I walk along to work declare
your absence, the headlines
declare it, the nation, and
over and over the harried lives I
watch and live with, holding my breath and
sometimes a thing rings true –
they all give way and declare your real absence.

Master and Lord,
let be. I can say
nothing about you that does not
vanish like tap water.
I know,
the world is not enough; a woman straightens
and turns from the sink and asks her life the question, why should she
fake it? – and after a moment she
shrugs, and returns to the sink. A man's
adrenalin takes hold, at a meeting he makes
his point, and pushes and sees that

things will happen now and then in the pause he knows
there are endless things in the world and this is not for real.

Whatever is lovely, whatever deserves
contempt, whatever dies –
over and over, in every thing we meet
we meet that emptiness.
It is a homecoming, as men once knew
their lives took place in you.
And we cannot get on, no matter how we
rearrange our lives and we cannot let go for
then there is nothing at all.

Master and Lord, there was a
measure once.
There was a time when men could say
my life, my job, my home
and still feel clean.
The poets spoke of earth and heaven. There were no symbols.

3

The light rides easy on people dozing at noon in Toronto, or
here it does, in the square, with the white spray hanging
upward in plumes on the face of the pool, and the kids and the thrum of
    the traffic,
and the people come and they feel no consternation, dozing at
lunchtime; even the towers comply.
And they prevail in their placid continuance, idly unwrapping their food
day after day on the slabs by the pool, warm in the summer sun.
Day after day the light rides easy.
Nothing is important.
But once at noon I felt my body's pulse contract and
balk in the space of the square, it puckered and jammed till nothing
worked – the whole brave willed design
an abstract pass at grandeur, and casting back and forth
the only resonance that held was in the Archer.
Great bronze simplicity! that muscled form still
moved in the aimless expanse, and tense and
waiting to the south I stood until the clangour in my forearms found its
    outlet.
And when it came I knew that stark heraldic form is not
great art. For it is real, great art is less than its necessity.
But it held; when the monumental space of the square
went slack, it moved in sterner space.
Was shaped by earlier space and it ripples with
wrenched stress, the bronze is flexed by
blind aeonic throes
that bred and met in slow enormous impact,
and they are still at large for the force in the bronze churns
through it, and lunges beyond and also the Archer declares

that space is primal, raw, beyond control and drives toward a
living stillness, its own.

But if some man by the pool, doing his workaday
job in the city, hammering
type for credits or bread, or in for the day, wiped out in Long Branch
by the indelible sting of household acts of war,
or whatever; if a man strays into that
vast barbaric space it happens that he enters into
void and will go
under, or he must himself become void.

We live on occupied soil.
Across the barren Shield, immortal scrubland and our own,
where near the beginning the spasms of lava
settled to bedrock schist,
barbaric land, initial, our
own, scoured bare under
crush of the glacial recessions,
and later it broke the settlers, towing them
deeper and deeper each year beneath the
gritty sprinkle of soil, till men who had worked their farms for a lifetime
could snap in a month from simple cessation of will,
though the brute surroundings went on – the flagrant changes
of maple and sumach, the water in ripples of light,
the faces of outcrop, the stillness, and up the slopes
a vast incessant green that drew the mind
beyond its tether, north, to muskeg and
stunted hackmatack, and then the whine of icy tundra north to the pole –
despotic land, inhuman yet
our *own*, where else on earth? and reaping stone
from the bush their parents cleared, the sons gave

way and they drank all year, or went strange, or they sat and stared
     outside
as their cars settled back to slag and now what
races toward us on asphalt across the Shield –
by truck, by TV minds and the ore-bearing boxcars –
is torn from the land and all those fruitless lives, it no longer
stays for us, immemorial adversary, but is shipped and divvied abroad.

Take Tom Thomson, painter: he
did his work in the Shield.
Could guide with a blindfold on. Was part of the bush. Often when night
came down in a subtle rush and the scorched scrub still
ached for miles from the fires he paddled direct through
the palpable dark, hearing only the push and
drip of the blade for hours and then very suddenly the radiance of the
renewed land broke over his canvas. So. It was his
job. But no two moments land with the same sideswipe
and Thomson, for all his savvy, is very damp and
trundled by submarine currents, pecked by the fish out
somewhere cold in the Shield and the far loons percolate
high in November and he is not painting their cry.

Small things ignite us, and the quirky particulars
flare on all sides.
A cluster of birches, in moonlight;
a jack pine, gnarled and
focussing heaven and earth –
these might fend off void.
Or under the poolside arches the sunlight, skidding on paper destroyers,
kindles a dazzle, skewing the sense. Like that. Any
combination of us and time can start the momentary

ignition. If only it were enough.
But it is two thousand years since Christ's corpse rose in a glory,
and now the shiny ascent is not for us, Thomson is
done and we cannot
malinger among the bygone acts of grace.
For many are called but none are chosen now, we are the evidence
for downward momentum, although despite our longing still
restrained within the real, as Thomson's body really did
decay and vying to praise him
we bicker about which grave the carcass fills.

New silences occur in the drone of the square's great spaces.
The light overbalances, shadows
appear, the people walk away.
But massy and knotted and still the Archer continues its space,
which violates our lives, and reminds us, and has no mercy upon us.
For a people which lays its whiskey and violent machines
on a land that is primal, and native, which takes that land in greedy
innocence but will not live it, which is not claimed by its own
and it sells that land off even before it has owned it,
traducing the immemorial pacts of men and earth, free and
beyond them, exempt by miracle from the fate of the race –
that people will botch its cities, its greatest squares
will mock its money and stature, and prising wide
a civil space to live in, by the grace of its own invention it will
fill that space with the artifacts of death.

On Queen Street, therefore, in Long Branch, wherever the
people have come upon it, say that the
news is as bad as we thought.
We have spent the bankroll; here, in this place,
it is time to honour the void.

4

Among the things which
hesitate to be, is void our
vocation? The houses on the street
hold back from us, across the welter of city blocks
old friendships keep stalling,
even the square falls away and the acts of our statesmen
will not come real though we long for it.
Dwelling among the
bruised and infinitely binding world
are we not meant to
relinquish it all, to begin at last
the one abundant psalm of letting be?

If only it
held. If only
here and now were not fastened so
deep in the flesh and goodbye, but how should a man,
alive and tied to the wreckage that surrounds him,
the poisoned air goodbye, goodbye the lakes,
the earth and precious habitat of species,
goodbye the grainy sense of place, worn down in
words and the local ways of peoples, goodbye the children returning
as strangers to their roots and generations,
and cities dying of concrete, city goodbye my city of passionate bickering
neighbourhoods the corner stores
all ghosts among the high-rise, like bewildered nations after their
surcease as boundaries
diminish to formalities on maps goodbye, so many
lives gone down the drain in the service of empire,

bombing its demon opponents though they bleed like men goodbye,
and not that all things die but that they die meanly, and
goodbye the lull of the sun in the square, goodbye and
goodbye the magisterial life of the mind, in the
domination of number every
excellent workaday thing all spirited
men and women ceaselessly jammed at their breaking
points goodbye who have such little time on earth and constantly
    fastened
how should a man stop caring?

And yet the death of lakes, the gutting of our self-respect,
even the passage of Canada –
these do not intrude such radical
bereavement merely to
etch us in figures of loss, to bid us declare
how painfully each passing brings us down.
Every thing we own will disappear; nothing
belongs to us, and
only that nothing is home.
And this is what the things were telling us: if we can
face the rigours of detachment, meaning our
life, our job, our home, permitting it to
break over us, letting it
bring us down till every
itch and twitch of attachment loses its purchase,
at the dead-end of desire and for some it will last
a month and for some ten years, at last we may
find ourselves in the midst of what abounds,
though that is not it but now we are set
free to cherish the world which has been stripped away by stages, and
    with no

reason the things are renewed: the people, Toronto, the elms
still greening in their blighted silhouettes – some dead some
burgeoning but none our property, and now they
move at last in the clearness of open space, within the
emptiness they move very cleanly in the vehement enjoyment of their
    bodies.

But what good is that in a nation of
losers and quislings? and for the few tenacious
citizens of a land that was never our own, watching the
ore and the oil and the shore-lines gutted
for dollars by men from abroad, watching Canadians
peddle their birthright and for these others, good
stateless men and women and may they go down in civil fury –
how should they clutch and fumble after beatitude, crouching for
years till emptiness renews an elm tree,
and meanwhile the country is gone?
    I think much now of Garneau, master of emptiness,
who in the crowded streets of Montreal
saw not lost souls but a company of lost bodies, and
moving into himself gave thanks when he discovered
nothing but desert and void.
And I know that appetite in my own life,
at work, at home, in the square, and more insistent every day it forges
outward through the living will of the body,
straining to reach its ground, oblivion.
    But some face exile at home and sniping at corporations,
manic at times, and the patsies of empire their leaders lying for votes,
till the impotence floods in their veins, there is
shame abounding and sometimes a few good
gestures between the asphalt and sky that might have been
adequate once, and finally dying on occupied soil.

Yet still they take the world full force on their nerve ends, leaving the bloody impress of their bodies face forward in time, and I believe they will not go under until they have taken the measure of empire.

5

It would be better maybe if we could stop loving the children
and their delicate brawls, pelting across the square in tandem, deking
from cover to cover in raucous celebration and they are never
winded, bemusing us with the rites of our own
gone childhood; if only they stopped
mattering, the children, it might be possible, now
while the square lies stunned by noon.
What is real is fitful, and always the beautiful footholds
crumble the moment I set my mind aside, though the world does recur.
Better, I think, to avoid the snag of attachment – the headlong particulars
which perpetually sucker us in, until they
lose their animal purchase and cease to endorse us;
this awakens the ache of being, and once again the lonesome ego
sets out dragging its ignominious hankerings across the world,
which does not regard them.
Perhaps we should
bless what doesn't attach us, though I do not know
where we are to find nourishment.
    So, in the square, it is a
blessed humdrum; the kids climb over the Archer, and
the pool reflects the sky, and the people passing by,
who doze, and gently from above the visible pollutants descend,
coating the towers' sheath. Sometimes it
works but once in summer looking up I saw the noxious cloud suspended
taut above the city, clenched, as now everywhere it is the
imperial way of life that bestows its fallout. And it did not
stay inert, but across the fabled horizon of Bay Street they came riding,
the liberators, the deputies of Jesus, the Marines, and had released
bacterial missiles over the Golden Horseshoe for love of all mankind,

and I saw my people streaming after calling welcome for the small
     change,
and I ran in my mind crying humiliation upon the country, as now I do
     also for it is
hard to stay at the surface one more time, with a queasy hi and goodbye
     to the char-broiled tykes of the Mekong Delta,
although the pool
reflects the placid sky, and the people passing by, and daily our
acquiescence presses down on us from above and we have no room to be.
It is the children's fault as they swarm, for we cannot stop caring.

In a bad time, people, from an outpost of empire I write
bewildered, though on about living. It is to set down a nation's
failure of nerve; I mean complicity, which is signified by the
gaseous stain above us. For a man who
fries the skin of kids with burning jelly is a criminal.
Even though he loves children he is a criminal. Even though his
money pumps your oil he is criminal, and though his programs infest the
     air you breathe he is
criminal and though his honest quislings run your
government he is criminal and though you do not love his enemies he is
criminal and though you lose your job on his say-so he is criminal
and though your country will founder without him he is criminal and
though he has transformed the categories of your refusal by the pressure
     of his media he is a criminal.
And the consenting citizens of a minor and docile colony
are cogs in a useful tool, though in no way
necessary and scarcely
criminal at all, and their leaders are
honourable men, as for example Paul Martin.

In Germany, the civic square in many towns is
hallowed for people. Laid out just so, with
flowers and fountains and during the war you could come and
relax for an hour, catch a parade or just
get away from the interminable racket of the trains, clattering through the
outskirts with their lousy expendable cargo.
Little cafés often, facing the square. Beer and a chance to relax.
And except for the children it's peaceful here
too, under the sun's warm sedation.

The humiliations of imperial necessity
are an old story, though it does not
improve in the telling and no man
believes it of himself.
Why bring up genocide? Why bring up
acquiescence, profiteering? Why bring up, again,
the deft emasculation of a country by the Liberal Party of Canada?
It is not Mr Martin who sprays the poison mist
on the fields of the Vietnamese, not in person, nor fries civilians –
he is no worse a man than the other sellouts of history:
the Britons who went over to the legionaries, sadly for the sake of the
     larger peace;
the tired professors of Freiburg, Berlin; or the statesmen at Munich, those
estimable men. And the lovers of peace, the brisk switchers who
told it in Budapest. Doesn't the
service of quiet diplomacy require dirty hands?
(Does the sun in summer pour its warm light into the square
for us to ignore?)
And then if it doesn't work one is finally
on the winning side – though that is

unkind; Mr Martin is an honourable man, as we are all
Canadians, and honourable men.

And this is void: to participate in an
abomination larger than yourself. It is to fashion
other men's napalm and know it, to be a
Canadian safe in the square and watch the children dance and
dance and smell the lissome burning
bodies to be born in
old necessity to breathe polluted air and
come of age in Canada with lies and vertical on earth no
man has drawn a breath that was not lethal to some brother it is
yank and gook and hogtown linked in
guilty genesis it is the sorry mortal
sellout burning kids by proxy acquiescent
still though still denying it is merely to be human.

6

I am one for whom the world is constantly proving too much –
not this nor that, but the continental drift to barbarian
normalcy frightens me, I am constantly
stiffening before my other foot touches the ground and numb in my
stance I hear the country pouring on past me gladly on all sides,
towed and protesting but pelting very fast downhill,
and though I do not decry each gift of technopolis I can see only the
    bread and circuses to come,
and no man will use a mirror to shave, in case he
glimpse himself and abroad there will come obscenity, a senseless
    procession of holy wars,
and we will fashion the napalm for our side, proud of our clean hands.
I can't converse with friends without discussing Rome, this is
bad news and though the upshot is not that I am constantly
riddled with agonies my thing is often worse for I cannot get purchase
    on life.

7

Among the flaws that mar my sleep I harbour more than wars for I have
    friends and lacerations,
brave men and spritely women,
whose fears dovetail and though often our gentleness for our beloved
is straight and incomparable,
we impose the roles that feed the other's hankering and go on to
savage what we have made, defacing
images, our own, and thus finally
destroy the beloved trapped inside the image.
And the nerve-ends come apart and we spend
long nights separate in the same bed, turning and turning as if
our dreams were real, for there are
few among us who are competent at being, and few who can
let our lovers be.
And some are freed by the breakdown, but many at once will
lapse back into the game, projecting our
monstrous images back outside us again, where we will
deface them again and again destroy the beloved,
and there is never any end to it while we are alive.

Yet some move through these hard necessities
like losers for awhile, until they
reach a kind of ease in their bodies' loving.
The agony hunger fades; they come to a
different rhythm together, around
the kids and their jobs, that allows for a
tentative joy and also for grieving together.

But mostly each man carries his lover's fate
inside him, which he fears as it stirs because if the drinks are strong
or the conversation proceeds just so it will rise up and contemptuously
destroy him, and at last when he meets the other
with his own fate trapped like a bubble inside her body
there is a baleful chemistry which draws them together for love and the kill.
And out of that horror of life
they take on the crippled roles that each has singled the
other to partner, the voluntary betrayal is
consummated and they are confirmed again
in postures of willing defeat, and furious at their own fresh self-abolition
they tear strips off the other who has been their accessory.
And they walk all night in the street for the fate is still in them,
and it is a rash passer who does not see himself on the go half out of his
    mind with the need to fail and be hurt
for these were brave men and subtle women, spritely lovers
who could not love themselves, and it is
hard that we have only
one life for mostly we cannot command the courage outright to exist,
and the months slip by and still we have not started,
and every year attaches itself behind and we have more to drag.

Faced with the onus of living our civilization, here, in this time,
do we also single out leaders because they will
dishonour us, because they will diminish us?
Do we conjure the ones we need?
And they act our hearts' desire for always they are
bulldozed by goddam yankees, menaced by slant-eyed gooks and happily
    there is
no hope that we might come to our own and
live, with our claimed selves, at home in the difficult world.

34

8

I come to the square each time there is nothing and once, made calm
    again
by the spare vertical glory of right proportions,
watching the wind cut loose as it riffled the clouds on the skyline, framing
    the towers at noon,
catching the newsboys' raucous cry of race in the streets and the war and
    Confederation going,
smelling the air, the interminable stink of production and transport and
caught once more in the square's great hush with the shoppers, hippies,
    brokers, children, old men dozing alone by the pool and waiting,
feeling the pulse in the bodies jostling past me driving to climax and
    dollars and blood,
making my cry here quick and obscure among many in transit – not as a
lyric self in a skin but divided, spinning off many selves to attend each
    mortal yen as it passed me – thinking of
death in the city, of others' and also my own and of many born
    afterwards,
I saw that we are to live in the calamitous division of the world
with singleness of eye, and there is
nothing I would not give to be made whole.

Hector de Saint-Denys-Garneau,
you came this way and made poems out of your body,
out of the palpable void that opened
between the bones of your spine – if you weren't just
making it up, you thought,
and humbled yourself again.
But your friends could only see that you were a genius,
and humiliated by their nonchalance as they strolled through space, as if

they belonged, as if their tickets had been accepted,
you turned back and fingered the precious emptiness, feeling inside you
the small incessant gush of the cardiac lesion.
And often you left the room when the party was
reaching its climax, and you had been foremost in repartee, Garneau,
and fell crouching upstairs in a sweat by the bed, sick with contrition, and
stammered out holy names,
destroyed by what was quick and sexual in Montreal.
But you lasted ten years more, in a suave vertigo
assaying the void with your nerve-ends, watching your
friendships go dead, your poems, nursing
the adorable death of the Son in your own imperious cells, a man made
empty for love of God, straining to be only
an upright will in the desert, until at last the world's hypnotic glitter
was made single, in the grace of renunciation.

But not for us; for the kids, and the calm, and the
endless beckoning things
divide us as they pass by with clowns, the tawdry
yammering goes on inside and it yanks us here and every
whichway, we are on all fronts and forming
new precious attachments and
often they stun us till what is authentic is obliterated, and heeding it or
even locating it becomes one more hangup, all that great longing keeps
banging back against the miscellaneous clobber of day to day.

And by these distractions we are saved, for there is a deadly route that the
    blood knows
and the obscure inklings of the implacable imagination declare it,
lonely among bedclothes before the light on Tuesdays;

and though I will not speak of where I have not been it is
the graveyard of many for want of the lore of emptiness,
which once was a sane thing, but now of those who begin
their lonely inward procession
I do not know a chastened handful who survive.

Catatonic exemplar,
cardiac, scrupulous, hagridden – you, Hector,
our one patrician maker, mangled spirit,
you went all out for fame and when you knew you would not survive in
    the world you turned to sainthood,
and you beat down the thought for the pride, you retreated to
Sainte-Catherine, watching your blood lap wide on the lake at sunset,
dreaming of John of the Cross, patron of void, dreaming of Jesus,
and you felt the ferns come muscling up through your body, the brutal
    ferns in spring, it was all
detachment you hoped, it was exquisite
penetration, it was
fear of life, the mark of Canada.
And now across
two decades and two nations, Saint-Denys-Garneau, my blessed stricken
original, still haunted by the
space between your ribs, maker and brother and comfortless, my
lone heroic starter: out of my own wrong start, I
keep my distance and praise.

The crowds gust through the square, the crowds and the refuse.
The luminous towers preside.
Of high detachment there are many counterfeits;
the world is itself, though sundry.
And I will not enter void till I come to myself

nor silence the world till I learn its lovely syllables,
the brimful square and the dusk and the war and the crowds in motion at
    evening, waiting to be construed,
for they are fragile, and the tongue must be sure.

9

Here, as I sit and watch, the rusty leaves hang taut with departure.
The last few tourists pose by the Moore and snap their proof that they too
    were alive.
And what if there is no regenerative absence?
What if the void that compels us is only
a mood gone absolute?
We would have to live in the world.
What if the banks of high-rise are nothing but
banks of dreary high-rise, they do not release the spirit by
fraying its attachment,
for the excellent reason that there is nowhere else to go?
We would have to live in it, making our home on earth.
    Or else a man might go on day by day
in love with emptiness, dismayed each time he meets
good friends, fine buildings, and grass in the acres of concrete, feeling the
city's erotic tug begin once more, perpetually
splayed alive by the play of his bungled desires;
though some do not salute the death of the body
before they have claimed its life, but crippled they summon
the fury from within, they tilt at
empire, empire, lethal adversary.
But I am one who came to
idolatry, as in a season of God,
taking my right to be from nothingness.

Across the square the crisp leaves blow in gusts, tracing
the wind's indignant lift in corners,
filling the empty pool.
People plod past through the raw air, lost in their overcoats.

I hunch down close to my chest and eat smoke.
    And when the void became void I did
let go, though derelict for months
and I was easy, no longer held by its negative presence,
as I was earlier disabused of many things in the world
including Canada, and came to know I still had access to them,
and I promised to honour each one of my country's failures of nerve and
    its sellouts.

To rail and flail at a dying civilization,
to rage in imperial space, condemning
soviet bombers, american bombers – to go on saying
no to history is good.
And yet a man does well to leave that game behind, and go and find
some saner version of integrity,
although he will not reach it where he thinks to, in the
vacant spaces of his mind – they are so
occupied. Better however to try.

For we are not allowed to enter God's heaven, where it is all a
drowsy beatitude, nor is God, the realm above our heads, but
must grow up on earth.
Nor do we have recourse to void.
For void is not a place, nor
negation of a place.
Void is not the high cessation of the lone self's burden,
crowned with the early nostalgias;
nor is it rampant around the corner, endlessly possible.
We enter void when void no longer exists.

And best of all is finding a place to be
in the early years of a better civilization.

For we are a conquered nation; sea to sea we bartered
everything that counts, till we have
nothing to lose but our forebears' will to lose.
Beautiful riddance!
And many will make their choice and eat imperial meat.
But some will come to themselves, for there is
no third way at last and these will
pitch their lives in the ranks of civil resistance, deploying
motherwit and guts – sustained
by bloody-minded reverence among the things which are,
and the long will to be in Canada.

The leaves, although they cling against the
wind do not resist their time of dying.
And I must learn to live it all again, depart again –
the storm-wracked crossing, the nervous descent, the barren wintry land,
and clearing a life in the place where I belong, re-entry
to bare familiar streets, first sight of coffee mugs,
reconnaissance of trees, of jobs done well or badly,
flashes of workaday people abusing their power,
abusing their lives, hung up, sold out, wrenched out of whack
by the steady brunt of the continental breakdown –
finding a place among the ones who live
on earth somehow, sustained in fits and starts
by the deep ache and presence and sometimes the joy of what is.

Freely out of its dignity, the void must
supplant itself. Like God like the soul it must
surrender its ownness, like eternity it must
re-instil itself in the texture of our being here.
And though we have seen our most precious words
withdraw, like smudges of wind from a widening water-calm,

though they will not be charged with presence again in our lifetime, that is
well, for now we have access to new nouns.
As, city, tower, hunger, body, land.

Earth, you nearest, allow me.
Green of the earth and civil grey:
within me, without me and moment by
moment allow me for to
be here is enough and earth you
strangest, you nearest, be home.

THE DEATH OF HAROLD LADOO

Harold Sonny Ladoo was born in Trinidad, in 1945 or earlier, of East Indian descent. In 1968 he came to Canada, where he published two novels with the House of Anansi Press. He was murdered in 1973 during a visit to Trinidad.

I

The backyards wait in the dusk. My neighbour's elm
     is down now, dismembered, the chainsaw finally
   muzzled, and the racket of kids has dwindled
to dreams of crying, *Tim-ber!* as it fell.
     Along the scrubby lane
  the air-conditioners hum, they
    blur small noises.
     Darkness rises through the leaves.
And here I am, Harold,
   held in the twitchy calm of the neighbourhood, remiss and
     nagged by an old compulsion, come at last
  to wrestle with your death –
    waiting on magisterial words
     of healing and salute,
   the mighty cadence poets summoned in their grief
    when one they cherished swerved from youth to dead
    and every thing went numb, until
   their potent words resumed his life and I, though
    least of these and unendowed
      with Muse or Holy Ghost, still
   lug your death inside me and it
    festers still, it
will not be placated till I speak the words of high release,
     which flex and gather now
  as though somehow the fences' silhouette, the
    linden tree, the bulk of the
      huddled garages – there but
   going fast in the fading light –
all, all have ripened here to ampler elegiac presence,

and the dusk and the hush and the
pressure of naked need
begin at last to coax your dying into words of wholeness and salute.

Five years ago this spring –
remember how we met? We sat drinking
outside at the Lion, sun lathering us, the transport-trailers
belting along on Jarvis, your manuscript
between us on the table and
what did I see?
A skinny brown man in a suit – voice tense, eyes shifting, absurdly
respectful … and none of it connected:
that raucous, raging thing I'd read, and this
deferential man.
Then it began: your body
didn't work   you had to learn it all
right now! it was part of one huge saga (*what* was?)
Greek restaurants
till 3 A.M. after class, in the cane fields
till eight and you learned to read
in hospitals the professors here
all dunces   your vicious unlikely family and
dead soon, you would be
dead and nothing
came right on the page, you went and
pitched the lot   was this guy for real?   then it hit, the
whirling saga
the table going away, the
drinks, the traffic   those liquid
eyes unhooding, a current like jolts of
pain in the air – I'd

never seen the need to write so
                    badly founded; nor so quiet, deadly, and convincing –
          and I was at home, relaxed.

              How it all floods back in a rush in my forearms:
          those endless sessions together, the
                    swagger & hard-edge glee.
       And as my nerve-ends flicker now, they do they
                    start up in the dark –
          the words I've waited for:
If any be rage,
          pure word, you:
   not in the mouth   not in the brain, nor the blastoff ambition –
                    yet pure word still, your
          lit up body of rage. As though …

But Harold – Harold, what bullshit! sitting here making up epitaphs.
                    You're *dead.*
              Your look won't smoulder on Jarvis again, and
                    what is hard
is when good men die in their rising prime, and the scumbags flourish,
                    and the useless *Why?* that
          flails up cannot furnish even
       the measure of such injustice,
                    save by its uselessness.
   And what am I doing, stirring the pot again,
          when every riff I try, every pass at a high salute
                    goes spastic in my mouth?…
              And suppose I come closer, come clean –
          what's in it for me?

But the friendship moved so fast; at the Lion, already
we were comrades.
That's how it seemed.
For I was drunk on the steady flood of talent,
the welter of manuscripts that kept
surfacing month after month, and often with lives attached. I'd seen
good sudden friends appear, two dozen savage hacks
descending like a tribe,
a shaggy new
community of rage where each had thought himself alone,
and claimed our heritage, not
by choice but finding it laced from birth through our being,
denial of spirit and flesh,
and strove we hoped to open room to live in, enacting in words
the right to ache, roar, prattle, keen, adore – to be
child, shaggy animal, rapt
celebrant and all in the one skin,
flexing manic selves in the waste of the self's deprival. And I was
flesh at last and alive and I cherished those
taut, half-violent women and men
for their curious gentleness, and also the need
in extremis to be.
They made good books,
and the time was absolute. And often we flirted with chaos
although it was more than that, for mostly I cherished
the ones who wore their incandescent pain
like silent credentials, not flaunting it,
and who moved into their own abyss with a hard, intuitive grace.
And the breakdown quotient was high, but
we did what had to be done and
we were young, Harold and sitting there
on the porch of the Lion in sunlight, drinking beside you,

listening hour after hour,
I saw that you made one more among us, dragging old
generations of pain as perpetual fate and landscape, bound
to work it through in words;
and I relaxed.

            Our talks all blur together. That soft voice pushing
      deep, and deeper, then catching fire – thirty novels, fifty –
          a lifetime of intricate fury, no, four
    centuries of caste and death
             come loose in your life, the murdered
        slaves come loose, great cycles of race and blood, the feuds,
             come loose the wreckage of mothers and sons in
  Trinidad, white
         daytime Christ and the voodoo darkness loose, your voice
              hypnotic and I sat there
      time and again in a dazzle –
then: quick change, the
         swagger of tricky humility – and then again, quick change and
              four days writing straight, no
    sleep say it *all*;
and then the phonecall – one more
         livid book in draft: from the Caribbean to
  Canada,
      the saga piecing together.

Driven, caring, proud: it was
community somehow. And your
dying, Harold your dying
diminished the thing on earth we longed to be, for
rampant with making we recognized
no origin but us …

But my mind bangs back as I say that, jerks and
bangs backwards.
Why should I tell it like a poem? Why not speak the truth?
although it cancels
all those images of chiselled desolation,
the transcendental heroes I made up
and fastened to the contours of my friends.
But more & more it's a bore, dragging those
props around, arranging
my friends inside.
    Piss on the abyss. And on hard intuitive grace.
We were a tiresome gang of honking egos:
graceless, brawling, greedy, each one in love with
style and his darling career. And visions of liberation
danced in our screwed-up heads, we figured
aping those would somehow make us writers,
cock and a dash of the logos –
oh, and Canada;
but all it's done is make us life-and-blood clichés.
Media fodder. Performing rebels. The works.
Wack-a-doo!
For this I tied my life in knots?

And as for you, Ladoo! – you never missed a trick.
You soaked up love like a sponge, cajoling
hundreds of hours, and bread, and fine-tuned publication,
and then accepted them all with a nice indifference,
as though they were barely enough. You had us taped, you knew white
liberals inside out; how to
guilt us; which buttons to push; how hard; how long.
Three different times, in close-mouthed confidence you spoke of
three horrific childhoods: it was *there* you first

gave blood, now you could use it
to write. And I was
lethally impressed, and only later realised
two of the childhoods had to be somebody else's,
and all those dues you paid were so much literature.
You couldn't tell which one of you was real.
But I can, now: you were
a routine megalomaniac, taking the short-cut
through living men and women to try and make it big.
It turns my stomach! Come on,
did I live that way too?
But leave me wallow in no more crap about the Anansi years.
Ladoo, you bastard, goodbye: you bled me dry.
You used me! and though the words are
not what I intended, they rankle but let me get them said:
goodbye, and good riddance.

        For eight straight years of crud in public places
             we worked to incite a country to belong to.
        But here, on this leafy street,
      I wince at those hectic unreal selves
          I made up year by year,
    and found I could not shed them when I tried to.
            Though how to be in the world?
      And leaving them behind
        I got here needing
    roots, renewal, dwelling space,
       not knowing how to live
      the plain shape of a day's necessities, nor how to heed
  the funny rhythms generated by
      the woman I love, three kids, a difficult craft

that takes the measure of my life.
Intricate rhythms of the commonplace:
a friend, a sky, a walk through green ravines –
and I am at home.
Though not to die here, fat & marooned, like a curled-up
slug in a dream of the suburbs. But for
now I am
here, Ladoo, here like
this in the yard and tomorrow,
and grief and joy rain down on me, and often I
think of those headlong years with bafflement,
good friends and deaths ago,
when voice by voice we raged like a new noise in the orchestra
as though each deficit we harboured needed only to be named
to take on public resonance,
and each honest word on a page meant news of another comrade –
like you, Harold.

But the books kept
pouring through your system like heart attacks,
nine in three years,
and the manuscripts rose in your bedroom, uneditable for
new ones would come and
sabotage your life. And
the life and the work wrenched farther apart;
you stabbed a man, berserk they had
doped your drink and you
went on brooding on style, your ear emphatic with
Faulkner, Milton, Achebe,
Naipaul, Gibson, Godfrey, García Márquez,
Harris, Carrier: these men you meant to

write into the ground.
No Pain Like This Body came out, that spare and
luminous nightmare and you
went back to
dishwashing, writing all night and flexing new
voices, possessed;
each time we met, your body was
closer to skeletal fury,
your eyes more
deadly and on fire.
It was all too much, it was gorgeous, it was
vanishing into your own myth,
and I watched bemused, and awed, as the circles grew
tighter and tighter, those frenzied drafts more
brilliant, and botched, and envious.

For I needed you, Harold, as
outlaw, rock-bottom
loser, one more time that
perfect outsider forging his way through sheer raw talent & nerve.
And I cherished that holy rage, I believe I
sponged off it.
Me, a nice WASP kid from the suburbs – how could I
live it on my own?
I could barely raise my voice if somebody stepped on my foot in a movie.
But this, now! this had
hair on it. It stank! It breathed like a ten-ton truck.
It bled, and it called for blood.
I wanted some of that.
And not just you: I mean
the whole chaotic gospel.
There was something in me that craved the welter of sudden friendships,

the unpurged intensity, booze, the all-night sessions,
even the breakdowns, the trials & suicides, and underneath it all,
half crazed,
the pressure of unremitting talent
revved up and honing in through
marathons of drafts.
It was a power source, it validated words
and the dubious act of writing.
But make no mistake, Ladoo:
I was devouring you too, in the overall
carnage and we did feed off each other,
you gave your blood at last.
I needed you to be the thing of fantasy
I now detest, as also I detest
the shoddy yen in myself.
Jesus! that gentle editor
with his handy thesaurus & verse –
out for the kill, like all the others
taking what he could get: salvation by proxy,
which meant raw energy, and the will to charge ahead
and live in words, and not ask any questions,
no matter who got screwed.
Say it: I used you, Harold,
like a hypocrite voyeur.

The wide night drifts and soars.
From here to the luminous moon, this very instant,
how many burnt-out rocketships go stranded
in flawless orbit, whirling through the
stations of mechanical decay
in outer space, our dump though once sublime,

the pleasure ground of God while he was Lord?
But they preside up there. And here – down
here is jumble:
version by version I shuffle images of you
and cannot make them fit.
A man should not make of his friends a
blur of aesthetic alternatives;
nor of himself, though it feels good.
Yet I also remember your sideways grin, the way it slid like a slow fuse.
And what was real was not the adrenalin highs,
the hype and ego-baths. Not only that.
Men and women were real, for sometimes
they handled each other gently.
As one spun out in the frenzy of his number
another would be beside him, as if to say,
"I do not take this seriously,
though you must … Keep pushing. You can be
more than this."
Beneath the pyrotechnics, beneath the endless
bellyful of ego, yes and even though
each one of us kept skittering through
the tyranny dance of his difficult compulsions,
what surfaced day after day was a
deep tough caring.
Quizzical. Easy. Frustrated. For real.
Allowing the clamour & jazz, yet
reaching past them, past
the very act of words,
to the plain gestures of being human together.
And I value the books, but now what fastens me
is not the books but the lives.
And my heart spins out to hold each one, to

cherish them entire, although
I could not say that face to face and finally
too little has come real for me, in the
casual blurt of day to day
the roots and resonance I crave too seldom cohere,
and it is only here that daily living half makes sense at all,
and I cannot relinquish a single one of those whose lives went
blundering through to love, albeit
ropily, and grew indelible.
And I unsay nothing, friend I must continue
locked with you for keeps in this tug of cherishing war,
but always now I return to the deep, unscheduled ground of caring
in which we lived our lives,
and the words arrive.

> *Great raging maker, Ladoo: go dead and legendary*
> > *in permanent regions of praise.*
> *If any be end, or*
> > *comely by excess of being;*
> > *if any be incandescent,*
> > > *on earth like me and gone …*

But still it is not enough!
I know words too, but when I hear your inflections on the
subway now I
turn and always you are dead,
nothing but dead.
What more is there to say?
I would rather spit on your grave than decorate this poem with your
    death.

And yet to
die, Harold,
that's hard. To die –
simply to die, and
not to be:
no more to
saunter by on the sidewalk, the
way a human does,
sensing the prick of
renewal each spring
in small green leaves and also the used-up bodies of
winos, for these come
mildly rife once more.
To be finished.
Commotion between the legs: no more to
accede to its
blurred supremacy, the way a
human does.
Nor to
spend your last good
muscle or wit on something you
half believe in, half
despise. Not even to know
the wet sweet tangled
stink of earth after rain;
a streetcar's
clatter; the grain of wood
in a desk the way
a human does. And not to feel
exasperated pleasure any longer
as flesh you instigated shoulders
pell-mell past you, out to

live it all from the start. It's hard,
I cannot imagine –
to be under ground.
And the press of another life on your own, no
miracle but acts &
patience that cohere: all that
sweet & cross-hatched bitter noble aching sold-out
thrash of life, all
gone as you reached it, Harold I cannot
imagine, to be
dead the way to be
not a
human does.

One drowsy bird, from another yard, and again
the neighbourhood is still,
the linden tree, the fence, the huddled garages, gone
anonymous in the dark. And though we
make our peace as man and man
the words haven't come to praise you – oh but friend,
you should not have gone to the island alone!
you should not be dead so soon!
But I'm floundering still, and every cell in my body
bridles, and tells me this is only beginning;
and I must brood against the grain again,
taking the long way round, interrogating
more than just the accident of who you were.
For often at night
when the stillness begins to
tick, or if I take on too many meetings,
there is a question, not my own, which stymies my life:
"What good are poets in a time of dearth?"
Hölderlin asked that, master of poets. Who knew.
But I just get embarrassed.
Alienation and Integration: The Role of the Artist in Modern Society.
Panel at 8, Discussion 8:30. Refreshments.
And mostly I believe the artists further
the systematic murder of the real, and if their work does have
the tang of authentic life
it is one more sign that they are in business to kill.
For a civilization cannot sustain
lobotomy, meaning the loss of awe,
the numbing of *tremendum* – and its holy of holies

goes dead, even the
nearest things on earth
shrink down and lose their savour –
it cannot dispel the numinous, as we have done for
centuries without those exiled gods and demons rushing back
in subterranean concourse,
altered, mocking, bent on genocide.
For the gods are not dead; they stalk among us, grown murderous.
Gone from the kingdom of reason they surface
in hellish politics, in towering minds
entranced by pure technique, and in an art refined by
carnage and impotence, where only form is real.
And thus we re-enact
the fierce irrational presencing we denied them – only warped,
grown monstrous in our lives.

A world that denies
the gods, the gods
make mad. And they choose their
instruments with care.
Leaders, artists, rock stars are among their darlings. And
to the artist they promise
redemptive lunacy, and they do bestow the gift but what they deliver
is sauce for the nerve ends, bush-league paranoia,
fame as a usable freak, depression, and silence.
Yet nothing is wasted. The artist they favour
becomes a priest indeed, he mediates
the sacraments of limbo.
For a world without numinous being is
intolerable, and it is his special vocation
to bludgeon the corpse for signs of life, achieving
impossible feats of resuscitation, returning, pronouncing it

dead again. Opening new
fever paths in the death heaps of a civilization.
And he names the disease, again and again he makes great
art of it, squandering
what little heritage of health and meaning remains,
although his diagnoses are true, they are
truly part of the disease
and they worsen it, leaving
less of life than they found; yet in our time
an art that does not go that route
is deaf and blind, a coward's pastorale,
unless there be grace in words.

But the role comes down like lucid
catharsis: *creator!* taking the poor old
world as neuter space, as one more specimen, sanctioning
mania and rage, the gift of the mutant gods.
And the floating role is alive on its own and always
there now, it idles about & waits, it is after
a man – who knows? bank-clerk, dishwasher, writer, professor –
and when he appears, he is shanghaied.
So, Harold, your ramshackle life
was yanked into orbit, and kindled, and given coherence,
and blasted apart by the play of that living myth.
Almost you had no say.

Galvanic art! new carnal assertions! fresh nervous systems!
          adrenalin ascensions for the chosen!
It is the need to be
              one, to be taken whole & alive
        by that which is more than oneself, sensing

the body, the
            brain, the being
absolved at last in a radiant therapy, resolved
        in single, emphatic wholeness:
to live on fire in words, heroic
    betrayal.
And I think of others we knew, comrades in Toronto
    who toppled headlong like you to the calm of their own myth,
accepting its violent poise like the fit of a new skeleton, all that
    great fury focused now in its settled gestures of being,
their lives in shambles still but redeemed by mythic contours
    and it moves like fluid skin around them,
    holding the
        breakable ego, titanic
energies in place at last, no more
    questions – or so it seems to one
with myths galore but no fixed will to inhabit them.
And our lives were single then, we were made
    valid, though wasted, for I
    know the thing I write and I would
gladly go back to that, gladly but
    I do not believe in it.
But you, Harold: you
    went and lived in words.
You pushed it past the limit, further than any of us
    and also you died of it,
face down, no teeth in your head, at twenty-eight,
    dead on a backroad in Trinidad –
    though that I believe in. But not
the vanishing into words.

The night winds come and go
and linden drifts like snow around me:
                    paradise row, and somehow it is
permitted to live here.
But though things fit themselves now, graciously
            easing into place and
                    are, as
            though they had always known,
that too has its proper measure, and cannot stay on
            beyond its own good time.
Yet in this blessed breathing space, I see that
                    every thing must serve too many selves.
            And we, who thought by words to blitz
                    the carnal monuments of an old repression –
we were ourselves in hock, and acting out
                        possessive nightmares of a
            straitened century.
                        Surprise! we weren't
God's hitmen, nor the
harbingers of raunchy absolutes; and nor is
            any thing on earth.
For madness, violence, chaos, all that primitive hankering
                    was real necessity, yet
bound to the gods' revenge and to
                    prolong it would be death.

People, people I speak from
                    private space but all these
            civil words keep coming and they
                    muddle me!
Salvations come & go, they
            singe us by the root-hair – to live for

revolution, for the dear one, for chemical highlights
for power for objects for art –
and each one turns demonic, for it too gets cherished as
absolute.
Even that glorious dream
of opening space to dwell in, of speaking the
first words of our space –
that too was false, for we cannot
idolize a thing without it going infernal,
and in this season of dearth
there are only idols.
Though how to live from that and still
resist real evil, how to keep from
quietist fadeouts, that I
scarcely know. But
epiphanies will come
as they will come, will
go; they are not
trademarks of grace; they
do not matter, surprise.
"Everything matters, and
nothing matters."
It is harder to live by that on earth and stubborn than to
rise, full-fledged and abstract,
and snag apocalypse.

Harold, how shall I exorcize you?
This is not for blame.
I know that
it lived *you*, there was no
choice; some men do carry this century
malignant in their cells from birth

like the tick of genetic stigmata,
and it is no longer
                    whether it brings them down, but only
          when. You were a fresh explosion
     of that lethal paradigm: the
                         Tragic Artist, *yippee* and
               forgive me friend.
But you heard your own death singing, that much I know.
          And went to meet it mesmerized – to get
                    the man that got your mother, yes; but also plain
                         wooing it, telling Peter you'd
     never be back alive. The jet's trajectory
               a long sweet arc of dying, all the way down.
                    For the choice was death by writing – that
                         airless escape
          from a world that would not work unless you wrote it,
                    and no longer worked when you did –
     or death in the only place where you wanted to live,
               except it christened its children
          with boots, machetes, bloodwash of birth and vengeance.
                    The choice was death, or death.
And whatever the lurid scuffle that
          ended the thing – your body
                    jack-knifed, pitch dark, in the dirt –
     it was after the fact; you had
          lived that moment for years, you were
                    already one of the chosen.
               Your final legacy
     two minor early novels, one being nearly first-rate.

I read these words and flinch, for I had not meant
to quarrel with you, Harold.

Nor with friends, good men and women, who also lived these things.
Nor with myself.
Though I feel nothing for you
I did not feel before your death,
I loved you, and I owed you words of my own.
But speaking the words out loud has brought me close to the bone.

Night inches through. It's cold. I wish I were sleeping,
or stronger, more rooted in something real
this endless night of the solstice, June, 1975.
Ten minutes more, then bed.
But I know one thing, though
barely how to live it.
We must withstand the gods awhile, the mutants.
And mostly the bearers of gifts, for they have
singled us out for unclean work; and supremely
those who give power, whether at words or
the world for it will bring
criminal prowess.
But to live with a measure, resisting their terrible inroads:
I hope this is enough.
And, to let the beings be.
And also to honour the gods in their former selves,
albeit obscurely, at a distance, unable
to speak the older tongue; and to wait
till their fury is spent and they call on us again
for passionate awe in our lives, and a high clean style.

.

NOT ABSTRACT HARMONIES BUT

You are on the highway and the great light of
noon comes over the asphalt, the gravelled
shoulders. You are on the highway, there is a kind of
laughter, the cars pound
south. Over your shoulder the scrub-grass, the fences,
the fields wait patiently as though someone
believed in them. The light has laid it
upon them. One
crow scrawks. The edges
take care of themselves, there is
no strain, you can almost hear it, you
inhabit it.

Back in the city, many things you once lived for
are coming apart.
Transistor rock still fills
back yards, in the parks young men do things to
Hondas; there will be
heat lightning, beer on the porches, goings on.
That is not it.

And you are still on the highway. There are no
houses, no farms. Across the median, past the swish and thud of the
northbound cars, beyond the opposite fences,
the fields, the
climbing escarpment, solitary in the
bright eye of the sun the
birches dance, and they
dance. They have

their reasons. You do not know
anything.
Cicadas call now, in the darkening swollen air there is dust
in your nostrils; a
kind of laughter; you are still on the highway.

RECOLLECTION

I remember still
    a gentle girl, just married, how she
drew her husband down, they had
    no practice but she gave him warm
openings till he became a
    cocky simpleton inside her,
coming like kingdom come for the excellent
    pleasure it made in their bodies. *ew.*

Whatever I say, woman,
it is not that
        I say our lives are working – but feel the
  ambush of soft air – nor that our
        rancour & precious remorse can be
surrendered merely because the earth has taken
        green dominion here, beneath us
            the belly of grass is real; and lady,
it is not that
        lovers by the score come sporting
  fantasies like we had, strolling
        bright-eyed past the portulaca – we could
  whisper messages, they would be
        snarls in our own blood;
                and I am
  bitter about our reconciliations, we panicked, we
        snowed ourselves each time. So lady,
it is not that
        I hanker for new beginnings – confession and
  copout, we know that game; it's as real as the
        whiskey, the fights, the pills.
And I do not start this now because the grass is green,
        and not because in front of us the
path makes stately patterns down the slope to Grenadier, and all the
        random ambling of the couples hangs
            like courtly bygones in the shining air;
        the old longing is there, it always will but I will not
        allow it.

But there is
       you, lady. I
want you to
       be, and I want you.
          (Lie here on the grass beside me;
             hear me tie my tongue in knots.)
I can't talk brave palaver like
          I did 10 years ago – I
       used up all the words – but now I
sense my centre in these new
       gropings, wary, near yours, woman,
          coming to
              difficult sanities.

      I want to be here.

I

Walking north from his other lives in a fine rain
            through the high-rise pavilion on Walmer
    lost in the vague turbulence he harbours
            Rochdale   Anansi   how many
        routine wipeouts has he performed since he was born?
                            and mostly himself;
            drifting north to the three-storey
        turrets & gables, the squiggles and arches and
    baleful asymmetric glare of the houses he loves
            Toronto gothic
walking north in the fine rain, trudging home through the late afternoon
        he comes to Sibelius Park.
Across that green expanse he sees
        the cars parked close, every second licence yankee, he thinks of
    the war and the young men dodging, his wife inside
        with her counsel   her second thoughts
                and the children, needing more than they can give.
And behind him, five blocks south, his other lives
    in rainy limbo till tomorrow:
            Rochdale, yes   Anansi
            the fine iconic books, sheepish errata
                shitwork in a cold basement, moody
            triumphs of the mind
                hassling printers   hassling banks
            and the grim dudgeon with friends – men with
    deep combative egos, driven men, they cannot sit still, they go on

brooding on Mao   on Gandhi
and they cannot resolve their lives but together they make up
          emblems of a unified civilization,
    the fine iconic books;
                    he is rooted in books and in
that other place, where icons come alive among the faulty
         heroes & copouts, groping for some new tension of
   mind and life, casting the type in their own
   warm flesh
             hassling builders   hassling banks
and he is constantly coming and going away, appalled by the power of
      wishful affirmations, he thinks of the war, he
hears himself 10 years ago affirming his faith in Christ
   in the lockers, still half-clasped in pads & a furtive
          virgin still, flailing the
lukewarm school with rumours of God,
      gunning for psychic opponents
  though he could not hit his father and what broke at last was the
     holiness; and he can't go back there any more
without hearing the livelong flourish
      of Christ in his mouth, always he tasted His funny
taste in every arraignment but it was himself he was burying.
And the same struggle goes on and when
      he drinks too much, or cannot sleep for his body's
jaundiced repose he can scarcely read a word he's written,
    though the words are just but his life has the
funny taste, and the work pulls back and snickers when he begins.

And then Sibelius Park!
   The grass is wet, it
gleams, across the park's wide

vista the lanes of ornamental
>shrub come breathing and the sun has filled the
>>rinsed air till the green goes luminous and it does it
>>>does, it comes clear!

II

Supper is over, I sit
>holed up in my study. I have
no answers again, and I do not trust the
>simplicities, nor Sibelius Park;
>>I am not to be trusted with them.

But I rest in one thing. The play of
>dusk and atmospherics, the beautiful rites of
synaesthesia, are not to be believed;
>but that grisly counter-presence, the warfare in the lockers,
myself against myself, the years of desperate affirmation and the dank
>manholes of ego which stink when they
come free at last –
>>the seamy underside of every stiff
>iconic self – which are hard   which are welcome
are no more real than that unreal man who stood and took them in;
>are no more real than the glib epiphanies,
>>though they ache to bring them down.

For they are all given, they are not
>to be believed but constantly
they are being
>given, moment by moment, the icons and what they
suppress, here and

here and though they are not real they have their own real
presence, like a mirror in the grass and in the
        bodies we live in we are
acceptable.

There is nothing to be afraid of.

Saying crabgrass, plantain, begonia,
saying Queen Anne's lace, devil's paint-brush, flag.

Time I was young I thought
letting them go was holy.

Quartz, saying granite, saying dirt-farm, outcrop,
limestone, fossil, saying shale.

Coming back who needs it – giving up the
things I never owned?

Saying city, chevvy, collision the sirens;
hungry, saying finger, saying food.

The Coat

I patched my coat with sunlight.
It lasted for a day.
I patched my coat with moonlight,
But the lining came away.
I patched my coat with lightning
And it blew off in the storm.
I patched my coat with darkness:
That coat has kept me warm.

Silverly

Silverly,
　　Silverly,
Over the
　　Trees,
The moon drifts
　　By on a
Runaway
　　Breeze.

Dozily,
　　Dozily,
Deep in her
　　Bed,

A little girl
    Dreams with the
Moon in her
    Head.

Secrets

Columbine is sweet,
And sweet alyssum blooming –
Tell me who you love,
And I'll whisper what I'm dreaming.

Far as silver stars
In rippled darkness gleaming –
Tell me who you love,
And I'll whisper what I dream of.

Deep as hollow logs,
When phantom frogs are booming –
Tell me who you love,
And I'll whisper what I'm dreaming, dreaming of.

The April leaves
    Are restless now,
Electric green
    Along the bough.

They muss the branch
    And mist the air
Like smoky fronds
    Of maidenhair

And itch the april
    Lovers feel –
That quicker spring,
    That deeper real –

Until our wingy
    Nerve-ends strum
Hosannas in
    Delirium,

While saplings set
    Their borders by
To strut some green
    Against the sky

And all the vernal
    Gunga-din
Escorts a carnal
    Summer in …

But when October
    Comes and goes,
And frost and longing
    Snuff the rose,

Will April leaves
    Still linger, taut?
Or else be gone,
    And then be not?

There goes the phone a-
        gain, 's OK, just some
   New Age huckster, flogging a
          course in past-life regression? and jeez,
     sometimes I don't believe this civilization.
Sorry, love, where were we? – no come on,
   forget the wash, forget the dishes my
        hand in your hair I guess, that's nice, and the gentle
flesh and press of your lips.
          You ease this nutty jangle … No,
   stay here, don't go up; he'll be
     out like a light in a minute. Come here,
and I'll be back in a jiff.
      See? something about the
Symphony, I told them go away.
     I love your breast when you breathe.

Funny, I still get the kinks when I touch you.
   Four years ago it was very
     abrupt, it was
    wildfire & new skin,
    and now it's got all the drag of day to day in it,
but I like it this way; it's
   for real somehow and still I get the –
damn! there's a dump-truck under my back.

Aw c'mere, come here, *come here* – sweet
   vexed and
   falling apart with laughter lady: never,

       until I met with
you
   and did consort in this dubious space
          where every
    moment is out of whack and yet the currents of being together
       are endless deep delight,
   could I have imagined such
        joy in the world.
And it homes to you, who
       give it by your somehow ease of being
   new room to frisk, and nose about and
though the thing's insane,
          the Sonnets were never like this,
   decides to stay; and while you
snicker at the footwork I'll just
     get the phone ...

I

Well: I used to be young and –
sensitive?! hoo boy, you know I
    lay awake all night and dreamed of dying,
        like any young man should. Felt
    good. Kept the sheets dry.
But now I trim my beard in a rumour of white,
      and my body starts grumbling earlier in the day,
    and I would not be young again for a finished Ph.D.
For the young keep doing it; they don a fearful
        abstraction, and deliver themselves from
    appetites and earth
        with geriatric haste.
But I, being lately recovered, choose never
    in thought or word or deed
    to totter back to the kingdom of the young.

    My driven twenties – why are they such a
    rueful nightmare now?
    I guess because our lives were abstract.
        My friends'. My own.
    They left out
squawky imperfect flesh and the way things are on the planet.
And though we were first to discover
    freedom, fellatio, zen, and the class analysis,
      like bantam Einsteins solemnly arriving at the
        wheel in '65 – which was
    fair enough, how

else is wisdom renewed? and often we made
brave lives ourselves – yet all of it was abstract!
For it served the one forbidden god,
denial of here and now;
and I honour high abstraction but never stop being
various, earth and companions! and
gritty, and here and till we can
cherish what surrounds us, loathe it and
cherish it we will only
oppress it further with all our heady perfect systems.

II

How did I
miss it? that
haltingly, silently,
stubbornly, home,
each mortal being announces the pitch of itself
in a piecemeal world. And
here! it was always here, the living coherence.
Not abstract harmonies but, rather, that
each thing gropes to be itself in time and what is lovely
is how, once brought to a pitch, it holds & presides
in the fragile hum of its own galvanic being.
And more: as it persists it tunes to
every thing that is, neither in outright
concord nor yammer but half alive on
all those jumbled wave-lengths,
inciting a field of near-coherence
in the spacey surround.

One luminous deed, amid the daily
gumbo of motives; a well-made
journey, or tree, or
law; a much-loved parent; the fullness of grief –
whatever: let that
flourish in its completeness,
and every nearby thing begins to
quicken, tingle, dispose itself in relation,
till smack in the clobber & flux,
coherence is born ...
So each live thing endures,
rife with the itch to pick up
currents that do not mesh and
live their concert – *each* thing, which makes for a
welter of harmonies, until those
jagged cadenzas of meaning
ripple like simultaneous fields of light.

And if a man could stay
clear enough, stay near and distanced enough,
resonance by resonance it would ease down into itself, coherences
cohering till almost he senses
the world as jubilee: I mean
the hymn of the fullness of being –
the ripple of luminous cosmoi, up/down &
across the scales of
orchestration in many-
dimensional play, here good now bad but
telling the grace of daily infinite coherence.

I speak of full coherence
in hope alone; I am not that
quickened attender, and have no mind to
loll in a blissed-out stupor,
while bodies are tortured or starve.
Yet though it is
never achieved in our lives it is
never wholly absent, for always we are
buzzing on the verge, excited by
urgent currents that fret us & rev us and
never quite jibe with our own and in a
piecemeal world, let this be what I
dwell in: not
abstract harmonies, but rather the
chronic, abrasive not-quite-
consonance of the
things which are.

And the jangle is hard, but not to be quickened is death.
And we are a botch and a warmup, although
I do not know for what,
and who tunes us – if it can be
said that way at all – is an endless vocation.

Over every elm, the
      half-light hovers.
Down, you lie down too.
Through every shade of dusk, a hush
      impinges. Robins
settle to the nest; beneath, the deep earth
breathes, it
         breathes. You too lie
down, the drowsy room is
close and come to darkness.
                Hush, you
too can sleep at last. You
          too lie down.

Coming be-
comes you,
little one:
rockabye world as you lie, and the great pang takes you in
waves.   Coming
becomes you.

With horses you come, with arabian
slather with jugular grunts and in
fretwork, in fistfuls, on Fridays we come in the
danger and midnight of horses.
Coming you come like a spill, like a
spell, like a spoonful of flesh in the
roaring, high on blood
ocean, come with your horses, you come to be played.

In after-
come, you nuzzle;
you nestle and noodle and nest.
And the ghosts in your eyes
do their long-legged, chaste parade.
Each time such sadness
hushes me: slow
ache in your gaze – nostalgia for
now, for now as it
goes away.   You're
beautiful, small
queen of the pillow drowse, and
rockabye world in my arms.
Coming becomes you.

Somewhere east of the moment, the
        gist of a radiant here and now
    awaits its advent.
It is not apocalypse.
       But in that
ampler place, which is
    never fully extant for always it flares in our lives and then
        gone again –
in that saner place, and yet
     the image of where we live: same
       job, same folk, same gritty
streets and destinations – somehow in that place
    the things of day to day
coincide with themselves, they
graze at the source, in their ordinary traffic they are permitted
    to move to a resonant measure, and a life-size
    radiance prevails.
And not to dwell in that itch and intermittent glory – what needless
    diminution.

Wide.   Wide.   And
wide as oblivion river –
anonymous in its billions, the
tide of the dispossessed
flows on through time and stays.
And how can we reckon such grief?
Some by famine.   Some by chill.
Some by tse-tse invasion.
Flows on and stays, for in the
economy of the planet a
docket of daily pain
is scrawled in the genes of most who are not stillborn.
Some by torture.   Some by
plague.   Whole populations
enslaved.   Or battlefield slabmeat, stacked in
giant steps to raise
great generals to glory,
and there is scarcely a pause to humans killing humans.
But facing that history tide of sorrow, blank and
wide as oblivion river, is it not
hardest that each anonymous fleck of demise
was one like us? Each sporting *his*
nickname; toting
her singular, wild desires; or
this child's eyes as it died, and the mother caving in.
And again.   Again.   And again, to the
billionth iota of pain …
The imagination balks.
To glimpse the sheer scope of statistical

hell – and then, to distinguish
body on body on broken individual body – is to
enter a moral hush,   wide and
wide as oblivion river,
till almost I could choose to not know what my lucky life is borne upon.
Except I must.

Downward of roses,
scumward of oceans of whales, darkward of stars:
deathward dimension of every substantial thing –

did you not have dominion enough? did men have to lend a hand?

I

Who, now, can speak of gods –
their strokes and carnal voltage,
old ripples of presence   a space ago
archaic eddies of being?

Perhaps a saint could speak their names.
Or maybe some
noble claustrophobic spirit,
crazed by the flash and
vacuum of modernity,
could reach back, ripe for
gods and a hot lobotomy.
But being none of these, I sit
bemused by the sound of the word.
For a man no longer moves
through coiled ejaculations of meaning;
we live within
equations, models, paradigms
which deaden the world, and now in our
heads, though less in our inconsistent lives,
the tickle of cosmos is gone.
Though what would a god be *like*?
Would he know about DNA molecules? and
keep little haloes, for when they behaved?…
It is not from simple derision

that the imagination snickers;
but faced with an alien reality it
stammers, it races & churns for
want of a common syntax and,
lacking a possible language,
who now can speak of gods? for random example
a bear to our ancestors, and even to
grope in a pristine hunch back to that way of being on earth
is nearly beyond me.

II

And yet –
in the middle of one more day, in a clearing maybe   sheer
godforce
calm on the lope of its pads
furred   hot-breathing   erect, at ease, catastrophic
harsh waves of stink, the
dense air clogged with its roaring and
ripples of power fork through us:
hair gone electric   quick
pricklish glissando, the
skin   mind skidding, balking is
HAIL
and it rears foursquare and we are jerked and owned and
forgive us   and
brought to a welter, old
force & destroyer and

do not destroy us!
or if it seems good,
destroy us.

Thus, the god against us in clear air.
And there are gentle gods –
as plain as
light that
rises from lake-face,
melding with light
that steps like a skipping-stone spatter
down to
evoke it,
till blue embraces blue, and lake and sky
are miles of indigenous climax –
such grace in the shining air.

All gods, all gods and none of them
domesticated angels, chic of spat & wing,
on ten-day tours of earth. And if
to speak of "gods" recalls those antique
wind-up toys, forget the gods as well:
tremendum rather,
dimension of otherness, come clear
in each familiar thing – in
outcrop, harvest, hammer, beast and
caught in that web of otherness
we too endure & we
worship.
We lived among that force, a space ago.

Or,
whirling it reins into phase through us, good god it can
use us, power in palpable
dollops invading the roots of the
hair, the gap behind the neck,
power to snag, coax bully exalt into presence
clean gestures of meaning among the traffic of earth,
and until it lobs us aside, pale snot poor
rags we
also can channel the godforce.
Yet still not
abject: not
heaven & wistful hankering – I mean
the living power, inside
and, that sudden that
plumb!
We lived in such a space.

III

I do say gods.
But that was time ago, technology
happened and what has been withdrawn
I do not understand, the absent ones,
though many then too were bright & malevolent and
crushed things that mattered,
and where they have since been loitering I scarcely comprehend,
and least of all can I fathom, you powers I
seek and no doubt cheaply arouse and
who are you?
how I am to salute you, nor how contend with your being

for I do not aim to make prize-hungry words (and stay back!), I want
the world to be real and
it will not;
for to secular men there is not given the glory of tongues, yet it is
better to speak in silence than squeak in the gab of the age,
and if I cannot tell your terrifying
praise, now Hallmark gabble and chintz nor least of all
what time and dimensions your naked incursions
announced, you scurrilous powers yet
still I stand against this bitch of a shrunken time
in semi-faithfulness,
and whether you are godhead or zilch or daily ones like before
you strike our measure still and still you
endure as my murderous fate, though I
do not know you.

RIFFS

1

When I lurched like a rumour of want through the networks of plenty,
a me-shaped pang on the lam,
when I ghosted through lives like a headline, a scrap in the updraft,
and my mid-life wreckage was close & for keeps –

    when I watched the
    birches misting, pale spring
    voltage and
    not mine, nor mine, nor mine –

then: a
lady laid her touch a-
mong me, gentle thing, for which I stand still
startled, gentle thing and feel the
ache begin again,
the onus of joy.

2

Nudge of her snuggled head
    against my shoulder,
cool of her flank
    beneath my finger-trails;
all night, all that
    prodigal night at the
tasks of
    passion –
sleep was the place we went,
    as the sun came through.

3

How
hooked I –
   honey how

   hooked &
horny; hooked and happy-go-
      honking – hey, how

   hooked on your
honey-sweet honey I
   am.

4

clean sheets

hot coffee in mugs

the woman I'm wild for:

   alive in the physical
   world – how come I

been away so long?

Yup, this is how it happens:
you do your half-smile, serious and bantering both,
and right on cue my insides
cave in, they go immaculately wingy …

Now it's all coming back.
We're apart six hours and there's this
gravitational yank across the city: I would
drive through walls to get near you,
just to be near you …

And also the way my body-glow
matches your body-
glow. Or how you flicker with
panic at being held – and I get the empathy bends,
exactly like I'm supposed to …

Been a long time.

I'd forgotten.

Gimme more.

6

Home-spooked
hotline.   Nobody's li'l number

one   Big-eyed
radium child on stretched-out scrims of alert –

you could go off in *my*
life?... Well of

all

things!

I see you once, and it
happens all over again;
slip me a
hit of that wonky grin and there's rumours of
other – adulterous jostle of
unlived lives, hot possible me's on the prowl.

And when we sit down to gab, I get
babel and urspeak.
Sling us some
blues & true con-
cussions, pure jive on a wire: we're pulling
seismic flips and goofball acrobatics – and we
knew it all along!

Aw but when we lie down, it gets
utter. I tumble
head over hormone blur in a
crinkle of selves, sheer
sprong of expanded us:
ow-*ooo!*
We love like a backyard concert of perfect strays.

That's why I wrote you this note.
Wanna hold *your* up-from-lagoons, your
beamed-in-from-Mars bits, too.
Wanna let your many be.
(… And how will we
play it? like Bird? like no-trumps? darling, like movies of
speeded-up weather?

Ho hum you
said – so soon attuned
to ecstasy. *Ho
hum,* as if to say,
"Two weeks ago we barely
knew the peaks existed, now they're
rear-view postcard vistas."
Ho bloody *hum!* – till I cracked the
hubris/satori code: "Already it's
too good to last   /better
tempt fate fast   /take it for granted and *past* zip *past* zip *past.*"

For months before we lay down
it kept going off, it kept going on
like blips & glory traces. Sub-
versive inklings of a way: the
way your tact and gags and libidinal gravity
seemed seamless in your body.
I loved the sense of *yes* you moved around in.

To me it meant (like a dare, and I got scared),
"The world didn't have to lose its tang?…
That deep, departed hunch of a life abounding –
that's still for real?…
There's plain brown joy on the hoof?"

(And then we laid-me-down. And got to know it.)

They
mock at me, poor
    sensibles –

"*This* time it's
    gonna hurt!"
But I can't

    change their pygmy
minds; sweet splash of
      dynamite, just

    graze on
me & you, the way we do, in
    late-20th-

century eden entry high.
      (… Rare old
rendezvous on earth.

    Why else are we here?)

When you present
    your body and being and
utterly, bright-eyed
      companion –

  and when we go deep into
      one another's eyes, and the
  swim of communion is
ancient,
      ancient and grave –

  or when you speak, not just of
    love but of
  impediments to loving, and even that

  serious caution inflames me: delicate
        scrunch of your shoulders,
    probe of your moral concern –

    how can such gifts undo me?
      Why does my system declare,
  Ha!
They'll never get out of paradise alive?

12

But she's gone – she's an
    ocean away, and

what is she
    dreaming?

13

Sweet christ, you are
lovely – over & over:

tonight I can nearly
taste it.   Track of your hopscotch your

quicksilver
trace in my

mind; wry bracketed giggle,
that triggers an ache at the

core; and over & over, new
sister & stranger your born-again

flow on my
tongue …

Why aren't you here?

14

So I'll cook some
thump & witness, raise a
bumper car in the dictionary:

make up a real-
life us,
at play in the garden of words –

  remember?

Not that we were good enough.
But there was this new and, yes foreknown astonishment:
somehow we were being actively permitted to live in our skins.

Those perfect
conversations, with their lazy
clarity uncoiling …

Skin still homing to
skin, confederate across a
roomful of chatter …

And fit of a life to a
lifetime: sedulous, incredulous, and OK downright
smug as we
basked around the block, two nerds in a blurt of summer …

Doesn't anybody
know? we asked – not about us, about
acres of luminous storefronts, *camouflaged as storefronts,*
the sky in drag as sky, as blue as itself,

and,

free for the taking,
all dirt & secrets of newly indigenous earth.
Plus our non-stop, gut-bucket grins.

Heaven *con carne.*

Hot po-
tato momma, got you in my

mouth all night.
Absenty

lady –
land o'

livin, I could pay my
rent all year & *still* owe dues.

Some kinda
stunts & wonders? Hocus-
focus? Hot cross

nerve ends?
Come on c'mon nice
lady, we ain't got all

lifetime!… Indefatigably adored one:

please to
appear on the sheet right now, called up by
succulent, shrink wrapped, wholly refundable me.

18

Eerie
articulations of

love-
space:

delicate
angles:

arousal.

Will I
    trace this

deft a
    space upon your
body?

Would you be
        here?

19

Wal, acey deucey
    trey divide –
I'm a guy
    with a fine wide-eyed

lady freckles too &
    squirms when she
feels good, I feel so
    good just

doin aw
    shucks
tricks an she's
    SOFISTIKATED!

20

Hey honey,
     it
sizzles.

Come closer, wanna
     see your
eyeballs roll!

Wanna
     tell ya
things …

Don't like it, just
     don't come
in here – y'

     hear?

21

Capo and
fret, the
comical flesh
arrangements – flexed by
what rare
air, what gifted melody trace?

One thing
weird is,
    blowing

highwire struts of be-
    bop-a-
longing for

    lady in her moves, don't talk this
way – patrician
    dancer, *no-*

body's
    trick;
and has calm, and yes an olden chastity and whose

    pleasure is
classic, and breathes.

Six weeks of
plonk & longing?

riffs of
rendezvous with you?
I'm here to coin new nerve-ends, fashion an
icon habitation, name of

be-when-my-reason-for-
being-is-snatched-away ...

    while you
    think some things through.

Oh babe!
when you come home, there'll be
mountains of hot patootie:
bow-ties and ice-cream,
could be a big parade.
And speeches – aw honey the
speeches will curl your ego;
talkin bout
lady of riffs &
backrubs, my lady of nowhere – said, the
damsel of cro-mignonne and the
life we're gonna lead
(big changes, chérie: *beeg* decisions) –

when you come home.

"Hello … hullo? Yes it's
me – no no, there's no

problem, I just want to
change your life. So

look if you're
free tonight, could you

live with me?"

    (Come quick and we'll install

wet dreams in arcady, little donner &
vixen we'll rearrange the

continental mindset as
fallout & dandruff, and

oh,
by the way

could you
please be my baby – my

baby, *my* baby –
tonight?

I said I was
"happy"? ... OK: so I
   lied.

   The forcible re-
construction of a
   life,

      caused by (woman, *deli-*
cado) the grave
      assertion of your

      pride, your need, your cells, your self-
donations in the dark – that is
      not, re-

   peat *not*
summed up by
   "happy."

   Try,
terror. Try, *what I was born for.* Try, *whiff of*
   zero at the

      core, in this claiming
sluice of utter
      joy ...

   Try,
how are we meant to live?

But if I
got un-

lucky once – meaning, if jiggers of neuron
delight flashed non-stop thru my

system yet I
had no hope of you, your

lissome stretch in bed, your
wit your gab your *areté* your life-on-the-line

embrace, sweet lean to graciousness your
curve in the mind your melt your fathoming goodness, gift of

wayward grace in a
giggle – if, I say if I

got unlucky for an hour and
lost you for a lifetime, one long

scan of dead
tomorrows if I

had no
hope of you …

28

Hey funny thing, I had this
dream I dreamt you
came back here,

alive in my arms – not even your spiffy
clothes – but then I
woke and the sheet was drenched, it had loved-in

holes in it …

29

Will pass your place.
Will think of us in
two-tone pandemonium,
performing the belly the breast,
performing the stations,

referring all calls to the wizard of waste not
want.   Your waist: your sultry waist.
My stupid want.

30

Multifarious dodos:
notably extinct –

gangs of ex-
es copped their snuff & split –

nobody wants to be nobody –

I just say I know you are fallible & gun-shy and still we could

occupy one planet

and look in tomorrow's mirror and start to brush *one two one two*

The angels'
cure for when they miss someone *very* bad is
malt whiskey.

'Dja
know that?
I never knew that.

Found out
my own way, special,
just since you

went away and to-
night at 2:48 A.M. I am
practising up being an angel twinkle twinkle mud

Awright,
     jubilee:
le's pull off the
     mirror.

     You're looking like late-night
heaven.
     You're looking like rain.
You lookin like four on the floor & I thought I was hitching.

I thought we were quicksilver, now you're a
     ten-minute
coffee stop.

Hey, should I
talk
sociology?

when where what how who?

All I
want, woman, is
crawl up your left nostril & snuff it for keeps in sexual asthma heaven.

Music of
methodist forebears.

Flesh inheritance.

I say these dreadful things for
what I got left, I got rites of
ache & legacy.

So I'm too
    "obsessive,"
        huh? Too "wired to your moods"?…

Tonight our
        spats come back.   (Oh yeah:
    Return of the Wandering Spats.)

And sure: you cute, me
        addictive – but honey, you
                ain't seen nothin yet!

I got heartaches in real-time. Got this
                separation from hell,
    guilt with my kids, I got

two friends dead in a year my
            gallant parents soon and the nights, these
    plummeting dipso nights plus the

planet's shot – you're all I got left to
            hang on to.   You bet I
        hang on hard.

And not just that.

Most days, I'm

not obsessed *enough.*   For the

world sustains – it must! – a pour of

joy.   Somewhere, sanely past

wishing, it

rides into phase with the

news of its own largesse.

And bids us partake, calling,

Hey, last

chance to

dance!

last shot at flesh and danger!

For years I felt that hunger.

Yet always what I

ran from was the hunch, my well-planned

life the barricade – until two years ago I busted up my

life, to instigate a

blitz of deeper presence.

Just touch it, before I'm gone.

Since then, I'm a

freelance lightning rod,

hot for *tremendum.*

Since then I tote the yen like a sanctified growth – but shit, how

rarely I sustain it …

C'mon, *you* know this stuff,

you're holy locus.

Don't say I'm "too intense," you jerk: you triggered grace-with-cleavage.

Honey, it's
so-oo heroic:

"hot for
tremendum."

All that leaves out is,
the drone of the rest of my life.

All it leaves out is
the doldrums of making a buck,

daily ego de-
bris, those non-stop misfires – oh

babe! – with a bevy of
red-hot maidens, bad trance of this

killer civilization, yeah,
the blahs the yays the blues the yack-yack-yack;

all it leaves out is the stoopit miles of missing you –
the (hi, maw!) muddle of me.

38

When you're up to yr
homburg in
hopeless, & the

damsel is not here –

what merrie cheer? zip zip no goddam cheer:

just
DIT-DAT-DOTS of biological/
ontological urgency –

pages of empties,
late-night lady reprise.

Pen-
ultimate lady, alive – sweet

skin and sesame:
why do we ever rub con-

tours, if not to conjure
shapes of what we aren't and

crave to be?…
Touching you I am

meat & pronto, I lounge in the chutzpah of
flesh; then woozy with

laughter and midnight and
caring, pure

carnal
panache – you, you, you in your frabjous parade –

how should I
reach for more?

Yet always behind you (this is
why I shy away), barely be-

yond you
is

nothing at all …
Lady,

do not be offended when I
go there.

40

All the left-out
corners,

faeces of living, the
lint:

show me a riff with straight-up ejection & I want

those in too,
and count on your body to help.

41

Inch by
inch by inkling: niche by hunch.

Rock at my temples; sheer drop; fingertip
grips & a piss-poor attendance record in the daily adhesive world.

42

My
comrade of the
ineffable:

let me take you
down to
logos:

pre-
logos,
where

stones stone,
light lights,
hurt things & people hurt and go on hurting.

43

Can't hold them together: —

We two were given to emerge
to absolute here and now;
it was plain & quirky, as
rooted in daylight as grass,
bright with its own green sheen and
when we go, our going will not diminish it —

And back on the planet, what news?
A single scene:
that 8-month child in Chile, electricity
up her vagina; the sergeant is
flicking the button; he waits, flicking & flicking to
make the parents inform but they *cannot,* they
never heard those names;
as well he knows.
                    And
again: that 8-month child in Chile, the —

Vertiginous thoughtface.
Almost the heart goes missing.
Yet if I
deny the slaughterhouse
world, or if I deny the luminous presence,
something goes numb at the core.

    But open-to-both is
    mayhem –
    nothing beside that child's – yet
    falling apart with static and
    origin   /incommensurable jangling   /what is, and what is.

44

Barely, be
mouth.

Mouth to self-
loathing:

*kicks in the
abbatoir* ...

Mouth to
jags of

awkward, un-
prompted joy ...

Be mouth, and after that and what about us I
do not know.

45

If not for you,
I would be homeless in my going through the world.
It does not
attach you, but I have no good
person to lie down in – saving
yourself,
and the persuasion to.
If you hold to our jointure, I will be
strengthened in the holding that I do.

46

Your voice on my machine – and
I'm totalled, I'm
totally totalled again.

> "… So
> it's me – Miz
> Plonk & Longing: remember
> the wet wet witch of the West?"

Oh
    babe, do I ever!
My heart so full of you….
But *click!,* and you stopped.

Doxymoronic
darling, li'l breaded klutzlet:
get back here yesterday!
Gonna amorize you over 25 years, got some
full frontal loving to spare;

long distance love to spare,
from an ache with ears.

47

Take me again –
    suite of longing, suite of

lies and
    take me again.

48

Sweetheart: you gave me the
gift of ecstatic be-

longing, which is a
real live

piece of
shit …

There you go – haring through
Europe with that

haemorrhoidal
twit, while I sit here hot for heaven &

re-runs on
flat earth and fucking im-

peccably up at
what pas-

ses for a
life?...

Belle beautiful lady; cardiac
angel; my

cystine madonna – thanks a hairy
cluster!

May you rot in Buffalo.

49

But was I in
love with you, or with the
    image of your

    layabout love-
play, by
        bed-

    lamps magni-
fied on the
    ceilings of Literature?

    (... Gawd I said, I don't want
Literature I just want
    you &

    changed the ribbon.

50

It is
          possible:

you could be words and tomorrow –
          colony

homage, *aere perennius* and you still yodelling back,
          "No, no, let them

eat *my* cake if they're empty," as your
          figurehead recedes into red-shift anthology legends.

51

Smelting head foundries of ozone gravity breakage I
ached in a space and heard Keep keep keep

coming like something in flames
coming like nothing

coming like words are what a man could burn and burn in, and for keeps.

52

We swam into
paradise easy ...

That was in the flesh ...

Now it's
clobber & slop and
drag the jubilee hunch through a
busted language, you not
here.

53

Why else do I squat like a rain-
bow bruise in the night, arch-
ing in absence to you?...

It is for
lust. And
not just you!
                    The
world that lay in blitz and bits stood

singlified to our ken.   And if I
let the damn thing go, that
itch of a glory norm –

how would I breathe, in non-ecstatic time?

54

Three weeks.
No call.   No news.

Whadja think – I'm blind or something?
You're choosing *him*:
junk male incarnate.

And wherever you are tonight –
half-sloshed, skirt hiked, on your
back in some famous alley –
you've made your choice.

You had a crack at
sheer valhalla overdrive.

Now go piss up a rope.

55

Okay, I knew it was wrong.
　　　　　Over and over I asked you,
"What about him?
　　　　　　　doesn't it bother you?"

　　　　But *oh no* –
　　it was
　　　　two different things, you said, it was
god knows what you said, you had all the answers …

　　　　　　　Moon come soon.
　　　Big old moon like a
　　　　　　　plate of dogsick, and honey I'm tired,
　　　　tired – I am so utterly

　　tired of this slimy ribbon of
　　　　　　　lies, wound round my
　　　head, my
　　　　shame my

too-long life to come …

　　　　　Let's kill this now.

All
   fall, desiring
      desire, I
         magnified her name.
This one is for lies.

    This one is for
  old-time-cheating lies. For
       $A=D=U=L=T=E=R=Y$ lies.   This goes out for
101 Lessons in How to Lie to Yourself – meaning, first, those
          oinks of eternal troth.
    For the lie of *her-husband-doesn't-have-soul,-so-it's-okay.*

    And on and on, the lie of a
        love supreme when we
made it *in toto* six times, the lie of a
          love made true by danger, memory lie of her
      exquisite alleycat grace the lie of these
        all-night
   riffs & jackoffs this goes out for
      months of a life gone missing, for
         scotch black russian cinzano this one is for
          cowardice lies, for
     touch me and *save me* and *us* –

Roadkill love.
Reality meathook ruptures.

You know I
put my life in your keeping.

Jugular mercy.
Flick of your barbwire caress.

Wrongly, I guess – but
you told me you'd hold me forever.

Venom & blues.

58

Fact: it was
         wrong from the start.
   Our trek through plenary
         skin and vistas, the
blastoff to lovers' clear –
                  those were
         snotty renditions of soulful.
   Furtive.   Self-serving.   A lie.

      But if I gain
         beatitude galore, and lose the gift of
moral discernment,
         how real is my rarefied high?
                  If I teem with ecstatic
   fulfilment but, bye-bye centre:
         what good is my life?

      Deep source, dire
   origin: my
         swarm of thoughts is
busywork, and what is real
         exerts its steady terror.
   The words are so much yack.
                  I happen in the spaces.
But when my life goes mute again, tonight,
         I have no place to be,
                  except your deep,
         except your stark,
            except your stern.

Maybe *you-and-me* was a lie.
But that big old easy place, where the

preternatural authority
flared out and, wham, it was

simply *a*
man and a woman:

that was
deeper than you-and-me ...

And okay, it's us that got mugged.
And a

lark and
a wrench and a lifetime.

But also, that
space of epochal

being is
shaped like home (even if

what? and *where did it go?*
are past my ken).   And now, though I

may not stay
bonded to you, by

reason of unclean union, still I
will not stop homing to

home.

60

It was bad.   Bad! It got
            bad, and
honey I'm sorry: I
                    lost the beat.
            That stuff was garbage.

But listen, your letter just came – and
we're gonna make it! got
                    too much to lose …

So let's go
    back to the good part again;
            nothing is pure.

Back to
            he plus she, and
electric ever after – please, back to our

                    tantric
    buzz, the eros/
                    lobotomy smorgasbord.

149

61

There were
coals of noel, hot bother & jeez, don't wanna

grab you for numinous stand-ins but honest to
edges got charred, fucken

wings half came off –
thought I was crocked & goners.

… Think I'd let go of
you, and heaven, now?

62

Clear tracings in
empty space:

from silence,

nothing to
words to back to back to silence …

I could go
drunk into

jive-time, the
emptiness, these halo lady

tracings.

63

Look maw – no mind, and
I can

stick to the stony face of
nothing,

nothing-&-
you, and inch a-

head for one
more chomp on the root of *is*.

64

Stir me again.

I cd be hoisted *how* high, I cd be
god in a handcart: BLEEP.

Even the speechlessest rockface deigns to utter its pendant climbers.

65

One week to go: come
soonest.
Have walked some
planks since you been gone and now
would love to walk straight up the plank to
you arriving.
"Take *that*," I'd say, and hand you what has
happened since you left but I would
take it back awhile, lie down and
breathing slow beside you hope to
ease your eyelid stress and coming home.

66

Burning thru
altitudes of lifetime:
atmosphere very thin, me
very too. Fuel for outward, low –
back, a farce.

Signal if you are receiving this, otherwise ciao.

There is a pure
over-
load, & it

copes
w/
modernity …

I want that. I also want
chaucer and
water.

Just now I thought to your
doorway, you opened we
stood stock still in mind.
You were going to say, You *did* come but we
headed through the hall and
stood in the eerie surround – it was
locked, recalcitrant wholeness,
so shattering I felt
relieved we could not speak; we were almost
unmade to be together; we did not know,
Should things start here, or end? were we even a
ping on the face of silence?

So now you want me dead.
                    I
get the message.

            For months you had me
        hung by the heels and
            dripping;

                    now it's
        haul out the
                    guts, & flush.

            So darling – Happy
        Returns! must be some
    anniversary or other in the

                    ghoul crusade.
        Maybe the first time you
            skewered me with your laugh. Or that deadly initial

        I love you,
        at dusk, in High Park. Or the soon-to-be-never-
                    forgotten climax when you

            dumped me, you
            dumped me, you
                    came back today and you

dumped me, bitch and
congrats!
(And

thanks for the killer putdown.
You butted me out …

Now I get to lick the ashtray.)

70

All that stuff it was monkey-grip jive your mean mean mind
who saw your chance and slid in fast you came for manhood
took it shook it trashed my self-respect – but you know I
never did like your body,
never those porridge thighs the spider scrawl around your eyes
right right every midnight wail about your body shape was true
those moves you made in bed old *Joy of Sex* retreads, my friends all used
    to yuck it up when I described them
and there was never a "sacred place" it was fake I winced at the slobbery
    gash of your mouth when you came
who was my hardon for living you made me crazy but I never loved your
    breasts
never drank your freefall mind didn't give me a buzz that talkie jive you
    really done me,
screwyou screwyou never craved your roadblock thighs your rehash
    moves in bed never did care for your flirt your flounce your
    paeans your mean mean knockout mind

"Please,
don't forget me."

... Please don't *forget* you?

Oh right: you were just about to
slip my foolish mind.
Thanks for the memo.

    (But tell you what.
    Stir the knife around – to the
    left now, a little bit lower –

    and you'll get, not just the heart but also the heights the pits the
        drizzling shits & fun fun fun on Yonge Street Saturday night.)

Revved with
contagion, mumbling my

other names and re-
peat: Don't *know* this guy, just some

oddball goof wandered in for the sandwiches,
    for the body braille,
        for the heap big miniaturized cosmos itsy largesse.

[Stop all wired systems STOP.
Abandon all forms of pig-out epiphany addiction.]

SKID skid, dopey li'l
juggernaut;
Molotov sidecar momma, wrench me a frog.

If you got happiness tablets throw some out the window way down
    opposite side.

Hey I scraped the
guywire limit – been so
high so long I don't know low from Lassie.
Ecstatic on empty.

(& if you are leastwise interested, think to
salute as I shoot straight past you CLONK go push down brown-eyed
     daisies

          Goin t'
                    psych-
     o whiteout count-
          ry, gonna

meet my baby there –

          She make a space I
                    be there: nerve-
     end wipeout, wired for sound –

Cash on my head, came barrelling thru off-
side splendours; fetched up
quaint in a dollop of hell.

          Humans cannot live here.

76

the stupid artillery of stars

moon a cold car-crash

snow piled high on the lawn and
me here sweating

face down in it,
fondling her name, and

puking   puking

77

Gone, it is
gone.   And I
make myself a lie, carrying on about it.

Time was I felt
clear meltdown in the flesh.
Gone: it is gone.

I could not hold to it gently enough; my
finger-clench blackened; the bruise.

                              Well now I still turn, turn,
turn myself on in the dark – but what is to be done with

this pittance, my leftover life?

From one half-wasted by
bourgeois heaven & hell, and some tonight
would crawl 5 miles to be (mildly) discomfited so,
so taut is their agony –

say it:
whom do I pray to?
what do I centrally serve?

The 42 years of a selfish, directionless life,
halfway to goners now,
with its jerkoff highs, no right to even blaspheme ...

Scour me. Scour me, deepness, before I die.

Blood on
  behemoth.

Tracts of sheer
  unness.

Abyss and
  interludes.

I did that thing, I just can't walk home straight.

Egg-
shell

a-
live-o.

Still, a
live &

living live-
o … Just

to be.

Piecemeal-

ly. Pang in bare
potency.

Get up eat fruit brew coffee,
do work see friends lie down.

Squeegeed in moments.
I am being squeegeed in detox moments. And all the

highs I can no longer afford –
irony, booze, hot transcendental crushes –

still throb like absentee limbs.

Get up. Do work. Lie down.

Rockface
    hallelujah.

Thought-
    high
emergence of

    foothold:

faithful

      : phrase.

83

No, please, not again:

Your voice on my machine –

and I'm
back in the heartspace of
lonely …

But the season is
over: season of
flawless idolatry wank.

84

Byword, &
byword.
In beach-flesh

depths are
beings, under stone.

Us too. I barely shifted the silt of a comma.

Am going soon, but meanwhile I can hear
what mortals care for,
instep and desire.
Tell me what you cherish, won't
just walk; give me lifetime,
not renege.
I have no other use. Living I flubbed.
But mouth to mouth I could sometimes ache into words.

Deciduate, on grounds.

Am *a capella* palp.

What oncely greens is a light in the always-to-&-fro.

In her … And
then we were home.

Our
breath bunched, the shudder – us

twined – of
(and if the) desire and the

planet
go on, the maybe tomorrows and

missing her   bad, though our

names and are

(written

wind

The dolphins of need be-
lie their shining traces.
Arcs in the air.

They do not mean to last. One
upward furrow, bright & the long disappearance,

as though by silver fiat of the sea.

NIGHTWATCH

I have been summoned to explore a desert area of man's heart in which explanations no longer suffice, and in which one learns that only experience counts.

THOMAS MERTON

Dark house. Dark night. Stac-
     cato skitter of cans –
raccoons in the lane.
And a flutterkick gust in the curtains:
nudge of the warm spring air,
blat of a ghetto blaster.
Lullabye, little mind in the city,
lullabye in the dark.
    And I could be out loving it, I could be
king of the night with a sexy Mensa consort,
gunning my id around town.
Not chewing bile again, not stuck here
wired on whiskey vibrato,
in the wreck of my fortieth year,
who never thought my life could come to this:
alone, in a crummy house, with a shitload of empties.

And yes, yes, yes, tell me anything!
Tell me they love me still – not loud but
so I believe it.
And again! There was a time
to plod and plod as though sheer 9 to 5 was all that mattered,
and those endless jobs were dues I had to pay: a way of
(say it) cherishing my own.
    But also a time for my hopes to come partway true.
Eight books; great kids; recognition –
                     and with that, poor jerk, I
choked, I flailed, I spun out into wildness, making

everyone's life the pits.
My precious career went far from me.
As when that night a year ago I woke in sweat,
and my wife lay locked and dreaming,
and in a pristine vertigo I knew my life had come apart.

For the years come
faster now – year by year they
come faster, and
pass me and
in my only time on earth,
who's going to know I've been here?
what's going to speak my name?
Empires go down: Etruscan to footnote,
Stalin to obloquy, but
what will have spoken my inmost name?

Which is the
thing which I
thought I would think about.
(*Clink!*
bright
cubes in the whiskey jostle.)
Talk about (*clink!*) the dream of a
brand new life in marriage. Brave beginnings, our bodies at
twenty-two like birthday gifts: the headlong
yes, for keeps – and how did the thing turn toxic? to nights of
cross-talk and loneliness, in a subdivided bed?
And not just the tiffs about friends; her
snaky times; my overwork.
It was more than that.
For there were lies in public places.

As if, across that bright-eyed, pampered generation,
somebody changed the rules. Ancestral certainties
of faith, and work, and marriage,
mutating to "lifestyle options." Values à la carte.
Full frontal freedom, with nothing intrinsic to be.
    And we did, we actually
swallowed that guff: Jean-Paul and Simone in Toronto – we thought
new paradigms came easy, we never guessed
there'd be a price to pay,
nor that we'd end up tearing strips off comrades and lovers.

            The dark is like a drum
      where fitful inklings coalesce and come,
                reverberant.
   And I must reckon up the catalogue –
         public and private,
     grief and gain alike.
So our long declension began, the years of
        trying to invent a he, and a she, and a marriage,
           without the help of old routine.
       The way that
          (clink) that,
    loathing the fate of women, and fearing the lot of men,
      she put her life on hold, and engineered
  small failures from great gifts.   Or how I
     spun my wheels non-stop to keep from writing – finding new
plausible jobs, fresh make-work assignments,
    for I could not bear to let my calling happen simply.
         That was "cherishing my own"? C'mon, it was
   total evasion.

But who can change his life unscathed?
Within our mental sleep we harbour
        nameless hunger pangs; subversive dreams,
which drive us out to touch a volt of
                jubilee –
I have been half unhinged with floating lust and intuitions, and for
what I don't know.
    So I am one who keeps the nightly rendezvous,
same chair, same glass, same tapes and
        why was the woman so hard? Lemme
                tell you why – I
            goddam made her hard,
through years of staying together to shield the kids.
                Our son at four, so
        proud on skates.   The girls, declaiming
                "Junior Bird Patrol," at the top of their lungs in a
                dripping tent in Algonquin.
                        Oh man! it could break your heart,
how they itch to leave you behind and still be your child forever.
                Me too; I want that too.
But that was a piece of cake, compared to the breakup.
What shitheads we became
(*the bitch! the bitch in amber!*). Until,
in a venomous trance and, OK a twinge of relief we
set the date;
        the pack;
                the move to this stately abode;
and now sloping through months of survival,
stepping lightly *cha cha cha*,
like a zombie on uppers.
Plus: the terrible pain of children.

And this I learned by living, and it has taught me
nothing I want to know,
except I will never inflict such pain on a child again.

Hoo, boy!
It does not make for a sculpted
dignity, squelching thru
catatonic days & nights, disguised as a
large, damp bundle of needs.
"Dignity?!" Tonight I could take a
half a million heartaches – all those cornball teenage anthems,
every twangy hurtin blues –
shove 'em up my ear and call it home.
Shee-it: I'll give them dignity!
Goddam-the-
biiitch heartache.   *Kiiids*
heartache.   *Twitch-of-an-itchy-*
crawwtch heartache.   *Pickled-&-pissed-in-*
Scawwtch heartache.
Couth as a donkey's armpit, the
maestro of maudlin,
boss of the all-night blues …

And up it starts again –
return of the lifestyle freedom options rant.
Kee-ristawfuckenmighty! let me
spew it out of my mouth: the wilful
amnesias of a criminal civilization, expunging
lakes and skies and species, retooling
genes and pesky folkways – unbraiding the
harsh and seemly dance of necessity,
till high on our freedom we soar above creaturely protocols

for we are the ones who can fashion new laws of existence, hot hot
hot in the mind of America;
and in a glitzy, thuggish time how does anyone stay in a marriage
when the one good left is the free-ranging will of the omnipotent ego,
and castoff partners litter the landscape like roadkill?

Ten blocks from here, the
midnight freight slides by.
My god, that
perfect bruise of sound – and my gut elides with the summons:
Come soon, poor boy, come
sooon;
come change your life!
High lonesome
long-gone trainwheel blues, and a brand new self tomorrow …

Who am I trying to kid?
"Modernity Wrecked My Marriage" –
that'll wow them in Reno.
"Divorce Case Shock: Nietzsche Named as Third Party" –
there's a bleat with legs!
What right did I have to be married?
It comes to that.
For I, who am not a vicious man, was barely here
for the ones I love.
I lived in another country: my mind, or
where my mind kept going,
where something thrummed and
myself was almost the music,
and the truer that place, the worse my dereliction.
But the children paid the price.
Their cause-besotted father gave them

174

nothing to live by, and I see my darlings reaching out for sustenance
in the city of kicks and neon, who can neither respect me nor
suffer me to hold them, for they know
the botch I have made of my time.

And truly, I do not know how to move forward now in my life.
What make-believe I clung to! That each new
job, new rush, new busywork obsession
could somehow fill the vacuum at the core – and
what have I achieved?
A lifetime of manic drift.
But when did I ever
hunch down? stay close to the bone? obey the promptings?
And when will I simplify this accident, my life?

       Room fades. Night
  fades. And *thwock* in the plexus it gathers:
      got place to go, know
          where. Pour me some real –
               me, sheer me of the universe!
      And here in the hush and slow dissolve, walls
buckle and hang and collapse; dust tangles with gyproc detritus
    till ribs of the building stand tall, they turn to
         dance me, dance me off my entropy leash.
        Blowtorch pariah!
      Am lonely volt in the stone-cold mind of jesus.
    And will not stop till find a point to stand on, for
I would rake out my eyes to get clean, get clear to
        Danger: no return.

But the high goes higher, in an
exultation of undoing I abjure

all shelter, not one messiah shall shelter me. Let there be onslaught and
demolition of selves, pure
yaw of foundations, overhead cave-in to blackout and ambush of stars,
till space expands in my veins, goodnight, good-
night old life and I shall be large, be
large in the dark over Asia – spiralling out
with a hue, with a man, with a
cry a human
cry, exist me to welkin, to firmament haemorrhage come,
wide in the slippage of time and
earth on your errands, far darling go
greenly, little planet survive for there are goths among the millennia.

Keep low, my
          life.   Be still in the
    cardiac sessions, small when the
              cornerstone gives.
        I am not my self, I'm
    foreign goods – things own me,
              I know that now.
          Keep low, little life.

    Nicotine owns me.
              Cholesterol too, and the sweet deadly
    booze owns my body.   And in my mind:
              money, security, fame – how many non-stop
    compulsions repeat their
              imperious tics in my ego?
        Even the dream of no-ego, of
              goodbye desire: it binds me and owns me.

          And,
        being: teach me to be.
              Not crouch like this, in
    cobbled time, in stigma.   Not
              freak on a leash. Nor
        listless in slavery trudge,
    captive, abroad, and mouthing the alien tongue ...
                        Yes, and the
    unstrung harp hung high, still dreaming what
              dirge? what rage? what wind-borne snatch of home?

Bright sunshine I must've, I
slept in the
lordy, my clothes.
                    This room looks
totalled in daylight; who would have thought
the nesting instinct could suffer such epic defeat?
Something about a train, I remember a freight train.

And hello, little naked brain-box,
shivering on the rug,
wagging your plucked and pimply wing-
things;
            hullo, you pink
replica;
            hallooo! little
soft, moronic, too-too-frisky omelet – no
fling-&-fetch today; just c'mere, just
act like a goddam mind . . .

Gifted with legs. With lungs. With
a luminous plash of sun in the
grain of a doorframe. Gifted with
time, which ticks. With a job I loathe. Gifted with
no more place to hide.

(And about my life, there was something about
making a change, and a leash and an
impasse,
            holy holy thud . . .

Hush hush, little
        wanderer. Hush your
   weary load.   Who touched down
once, once, once in America –
and over you flashed the net!
And they said, You will forget your name and
        your home and
it was so: already I had forgotten.

      But how did I come to be here?
         This place is not my place,
   these ways are not my ways.   I
    do not understand their
consumer index; their *life-style options*; their *bottom line* –
        weird abstract superstitions, and
   when I settled in to stay,
     it felt unclean.

      But that was a life ago.
    For I flourished, I
        paddled in silks; I
   wagged my tail for pay.
I poured sweet liqueurs on my tongue, and cried,
    Here's to the old ways,
        here's to our roots …
   What have I sunk to?

Though they hem me with filigree,
this is not my country.
Though I bask on a diamond leash it is not my home.
But what am I doing here still, how long will I
desecrate the name?
who was born to
another estate, in a
place I have nearly forgotten.

Back with the scotch in the dark – how many
nights this way, old pal?
Lost in a judgement sweat, the rocky
tapes & jeremiads and around it goes again, *Y' gonna hafta*
serrve some-body; thankin
yew Mister Dylan.
    But it's out past words, to the thrash of calamity midnight,
where the bass line skids like a whip, like
acetylene balm, like a liquid wisp of forever and
what am I being?
Lost in the dark, with a slam-bang case of extremis.
Lost in my molten body, a Molotov handful and from this instant I swear
I can change! I can change! tip it
               over and momma keep smokin that bitch guitar.
    Got a cache of christened bullets, one for each
          pygmy self that lessens me, *crack!* – and
   tonight, tonight I'm contagious, tonight I could
             peel the lies out loud;
though where in my life is there blessing? and where in the world?

Old payoffs dissolve, in the crunch of letting go.
Codes of intent, whole plausible repertoires fold.
    So. The dream of possessions expires, in a flatulent cackle –
and what did I think, that a man could be saved by commodities?
I swore it wasn't true but the lap-tops and tape-decks pour
through me, buy me off
easy, wave upon wave in the headlong race to thing heaven …
(Slowhand riffs, like
          feathers of pain in the dark.)

And payoffs at work dissolve:
twenty years of editing, and for
what? a few good books and people aside, to drudge in the sewers of ego,
of back-biting, back-scratching, spleen, and all to
speed the canonization of mediocrity as a national literature –
was that worth half my lifetime?
Let it go. It was one more lie.
    And listen, I had this friend,
and for years I watched as he railed at our moral decay; we were
all on the make, or the take – I watched as the raging perfectionist
succumbed to a niggling success,
and the long, slow, lucrative slide to wised-up irony.
Sweet dreams in cynic hell, you curdled dreamer.
    And applause of my scribbling peers dissolves, glad
hand of the also-rans;
I hankered for comrades but the tribe was founded on lies, and
dissolves the fellowship of failed ambition, bonhomie of
bile and abandoned ideals and how often I too went
whoring after approval,
forsaking the bedrock claim of the real for a mess of recognition,
the trophies of sellout.
Old shopworn camerados, who am I to judge you?

            So, year by year and
                    numbed by success I went
            wired to heavy mirages, a litter of
        two-bit personae, till finally
                    shucked & plucked & dismantled I
            hunker at last in my body,
        and if there is even the ghost of a resonant *I* in the
                    blah-blah ego brigade I

cannot locate it, and lucid and pissed in a small room
how have I come to this?

And the dream-on salvation sorties dissolve, flukes of
auto-hypnosis and causes I leeched off, dissolve the inveterate
lies of a bankrupt marriage, dissolve my other vocation of
nurture for often I used the quicksilver empathy leadings to
get myself liked, a sensitive doormat, a moral eunuch and
dissolve and dissolve this knee-jerk curse and litany of dissolution –
I have collaborated in the falsification of my life
till spinny in gone light often I howl in myself, call down a
lethal wrath in the veins, move on, move on
oh mother mother was it for this you bore me?
And this I achieved in Canada, where I came by
generations of flesh and methodists to lucid dead-end,
though once I was whirled about and gorged on the
rumours of God I reached a voluptuous
make-believe, but better now to
drink the night to the dregs than drift in anaesthetic glory.

But I will say this.
It was
heart's largesse, to have lived a space on earth.
How precious the rain. And the pines. And the
night winds too, they were precious,
combing the houses' hair.
I have stood hushed to the quick: tethered by
rockface and boulder – mute jut of
molecular non-intent.
Or slash of raw sumach, scarlet past
scarlet in mind. And the merest

cloud changes, ten trillion per hour.
Everywhere, everywhere the harsh stark exquisite
                    tug of creature adherence;
    I am no wilderness scout but there is a bodily homing which
                    I too was permitted to know.

But it's back to the shame and the
scotch, for as a citizen I
reneged. While my city slid to manhattan,
I stood by and clucked. And when the country, my beautiful
gutless Canada, lay back
and spread for a star-spangled buck,
in the time of the great betrayal, Mulroney ascendant,
I signed a crummy petition.
    We cannot turn history back on itself but surely a
man can do more than watch, as the planet slides to ratshit.
Fat chance! for while we went
lurching towards apocalypse, old
mother adieu in the cradle and starfield of eons,
I wrote some cheques, and hoped it would all go away …
                    Tippytoe! Tippytoe! I may not know what
    human is, but I can say *No*;
            I can say No to you, and you with your ostrich denials and
deeper, bury me deeper – I can say,
            Creature world, extinct;
                    I can say, *Planet go nuclear come.*
                                                    And
        deeper, wedge me down deeper, nobody has to see me;
pretty please, just a little bit deeper …

When did it all go by?
The scotch is gone. My body's shot. And the years come

184

faster now, year by year they
          come faster and
              pass me with their cargo of bald spots and coronary alerts.
                    I have squandered whole decades, it's
late too late to start and yet too
soon to pack it in and one day, looking back
at the sum of my time on earth, bearing down
as the pain or the drug allows, half-claimed already
by the long goodbye and leakage of the grave,
what will I have that rings true?
"You're born; you jack off; you die – what
more, little window-shopper?"

              Sweet jesus, it's
         hard.   Hard to
            sit and accept – there is nothing more to imagine,
                right now is my life; and also, how
      empty the night gets.
           Night after night it gets
  empty, for I keep
        trying to heed the voice, and follow, and
           yes –
    but then there is nothing to hold,
                  and nobody holds me …
      How late I reached the place of no excuse.
            How late I learned to ask, what does my
      animal heart require?

But tonight,
in the lash and ebb and echo of the music,
the years and years a shambles, every
goal I chased a bad taste in my mouth – tonight

let it all go by, and carry me home.
Just let me
cease with honour once, where silver
birches tumble back to compost glory,
pain of the hunted recedes,
tall buildings tilt at last to their bed of
gravity, old men their
deaths and benedictions – all my
failures corkscrewing gently to rest, absolved,
absolved in the entropy pull,
as each creature is allowed its
downward momentum, and it is
seemly to lie in the place of oblivion.
Let me go home at last, and
if I do not rise again to the daily grind and betrayals,
all will be well, and the
night will be well, and every
journey into endings will be well.

We know a place to be.
It is not the same
for all, yet for each there is
one subcutaneous claiming: the place we belong to,
where our humanness is home.   And it is more an
exquisite taunt than a dwelling, for mostly we scruff along
by scotching the hints and traces – and how should we
honour that place? It is hard enough to get by.
And there are places I love, but when I found the one that owned me
it was nothing I knew. For in my twenties, god help me I
blundered into a –
what? A luminous tumult. Where I went in my body's mind. Not knowing
what that place could be, yet sensing
swivel and carom and thud I called it
cadence, more flex than content and
us in it. Feeling the current
snake through my life like a leghold rumble of *is*.
Though all the words are wrong – the place was
not a "place," nor a "thing," and the going was not in my
"mind" and I didn't "go" there – still,
tumble and source and
vocation, and in that hush and quake of almost-words,
cadence is iffy but utter, preemptive, you
come or you go but you
do not possess it.   It is
given and gift, a daily grace of
what.   And
what I know of being claimed, and home, and thank you,
is drenched with that sojourn.

And it was there I spent myself, day after day, in my thirties, obscurely,
gone now, and it nearly took me apart
to weather the pang transitions,
for when I emerged half out of my tree I was
nowhere, I could not find good
distance with others – craving too hothouse a
union or blah from adrenalin crash and that
        herky-jerky to-&-fro
  abrades a marriage; I came unstuck; I got frantic I
        went to live in career, for I could not honour the stillness
            in worship or in words –
what claimed me, unfitted me. And then it deserted me.
Yet when I was present to presence
there was nowhere else to be, and when not
it felt like betrayal.
As tonight it does also.

How late, my
life, will I
graze in the malls of America,
crippled by plenty?   How
long will I put off the time?

For years I thought I was
gold, gold in a
secret place – and
one day, incognito,
the prince my soul would come and steal me away.

Fairy tales! a blanket of
fairy tales!
But there are great uncaring
spaces, and the winds whip through from there and
pick us bare.

(Gingerly.
Soberly.
Home – in
a torrent of
riddance!)

And so I came to,
and I cried, It is time to get shy of America,
time to move out of here.
We do not need these burnt-out dreams infesting our lives.
I will quit them, before I die.

One more
morning, god can I
fake it?   Out the window:
yards of blue
sky in my eye, some kind of birds with their
yattatta birdcalls, dump-loads of light on St. Clair and
the traffic the
numbness the shakes.
And it's off to work we go, with a smile and a
nervous system.

But what a
thick, benighted passel of hash is a man
with a hangover. Host to
cacophony – as now, for while he ghosts through his body's doldrums
he also feels the reverb: last night still going off, the highs a welter of
banshees in echo park; today's bad-news-to-come
a backward spreading bruise, the meetings and paperwork and
already it is too much, and day after day it goes on.
     But last night I lay, oh man, I lay last night
while the music spun out into healing,
and in that extra hush I saw – what
was it? – I saw that
we are the ones who need not be. And can only be once.
Born kicking. Raised in the little round
of sun-up and labour and sleep. And then,
phhht! – and never to be again.
One short bright blaze, between a dark and a darkness.
     And though there are different clocks for the things which are,

the poplars and mountains superb in their separate durations,
and Andromeda burns on a longer fuse, a supergalactic
blip in the lifespan of cosmos,
yet we are all, all of us gifted with
coming and ceasing to be,
in the beautiful one-shot pride of our physical bodies, and
precious enough to die.

And as I lay intent the jangle of time went to
radiance, I felt the glow of
my own life, my dear ones, the species and planets like motes –
quick indelible moments, of each thing being itself:
ping of our one-way glory, each quirky act and instant
alive in its intricate timbre, gusto or heartbreak or
rarer indigenous wave-length, each irreplaceable being
a whoop, a whoop! in the world –
and curled in myself like a foetus, I cried till I slept.

That was last night, and this morning
a vision and 50 cents will get me a *Star.*
And my life's not right, and
the light's too bright; and this should
not be the constant condition
in which a man goes about his daily ways in the world.

When first we came to this land,
there was a promise   a beacon   a
city on a hill, white clapboard new
              zion perpetual lookout;
                        and in the streets, a rhythm and deals.
    Lashings of brave blue sky – of gunplay and God,
              high on a noose of glory.
              It took us in.
    Cheap beer. New paradigms.   And we came
              pelting down the street
    when we heard that dirty beat, crying,
America, land of pure real estate!
                    imperial vista!   republic of raw material!
    America turn us to gold …

    Now: grain rots in the inland harbours.
    And far in the boondocks, the empire prescribes a regime
              of torture & famine,
              famine & torture,
    while here in the heartland the immaterial senses
              atrophy, grown over. Yet in the
    generations of our captivity, we bragged of our miniscule perks;
              in the years of our exile we
    scoffed at the rumours of home,
crediting only, USA/America   USSR/America   Babylon planet.
         Though in the end we stammer, *Earth, green earth and*
              dying: in our
              lifetime, maybe,
                    goodbye.

Mostly we have to keep low.
But also it's good to come to be hunger pangs,
taking the
shape sheer craving makes. And it will go
hard with those who have found their ease in America.
I will come out.
For there is a calling, nameable by silence; and a
track, a path of no-
going. There is an
exodus, though mainly
one by one by one.   *I will come out.*
Whose price is my life.
And though my tongue is blind, and I balk and have no maps *I
will come out.*

1

Over me, over
                me, oak leaves.
Dusk thickens by degrees.
Be well, great headfuls of night,
                above my commotion;
I will not settle now for less than everything.

2

The thing I was hot for,
                I squandered.
And the thing I walked past, I
now crave.
                Home again home
again – that's how
it goes, it goes
by and you miss the one you could barely wait to tell goodbye.

3

Funny, how a heart
                can turn a feast to
        famine.   There I was: hot
crotch and a taste for forever,

cloud nine on a crosswalk ...
Aw, but I'm
too far headed; I'm
bye-bye buddha, I'm gone.

4

Electric DT's of late-night unfulfilment, riffs of
she by impossible she – why was it so urgent to stay
hobbled to eros highs and the exquisite, long-distance mope?

Oh man! It didn't have to be lived! It was
so much safer that way.

5

"Yes" in a life,
like bounty in a rose,
occurs and goes –

season of
headlong grace, and
then goodbye –

and what remains is
afterwards, and
coping –

6

The day insists awhile. And then
lets go its fleabite promptings;
small gnats unzip the dark.

And this is what it comes to.
Lone bone.   Mouthful of need.
Hominid toddler.

But I will not scotch my wrecks and blunders past the season;
nor magnify my
nought, beyond its time.

7

A day and a
day, and I will
keep silent; a
day and I will praise.
Gonna knock these
blues around – you know the sun still
shines, the night wind
breathes my name.

8

Across the street, a clutch of kids
dissolves.   "G'NIGHT"   "G'NIGHT"
The scene could be unwinding
blindfold, in a memory overlay.
The trudge through brimful dusk; the volleyed injunctions;
the cry and reply, *G'night,* becoming
faint as pals recede, the way it did in June
a lifetime ago, on Dunedin Drive in Etobicoke,
when I was a likely squirt with a headful of dreams;
and that other dimension, the stillness, came sifting through.

9

Like an arm. Like a
leg. Like a transplant.
I thought it went on and on, and then you
ran out of things to let go of.
I never knew
the midlife meltdown ends – and
still like a leftover leg you
slog on till you, inch-
wise you
make it to *phew!*

10

Star in your eye, little inchling.
Kickapoo nova:
snuffed and begun.

11

The names the names the names
till the namesaying ends.

I could say tacit a firm:
light of a no-light.

But hunker the wordless, the nub.
Hunker and ear.

12

Waiters and bankrupts, cops and illuminati,
Tories and Sikhs and depressives …
And I guess there's room
for a member-at-large on the sidewalk –
a seeker without belief, who keeps
turning around. Not knowing what
fastens him now, for the city comes teeming
with scumbags and wonders, all cruising for
home in his heart and in the wide world also there are signs
of glory extant, and signs of
evil in control;
and he will never meet them unmixed, nor make them be one.

13

Tell the ones you love, you
love them;
tell them now.
For the day is coming, and also the night will come,
when you will neither say it, nor hear it, nor care.
Tell the ones you love.
I have lost many who mattered, and I will say it again:
tell the ones you love, you love them.
Tell them today.

14

Full of aught, full of if, full of empty,
fraught with beginnings, and lucky to be alive –

nobody's child in the heart-held silt of the century:
ferry the greening and grief to bare-bones extempore home.

15

Words, words, words! How have I lived, if not by you?
Not by sense alone. Nor audible sounds, although I love them.
It is the sub-linguistic
seethe – half veiled/half opening – you
dislocate me into. Which
stakes me out, which lures me. I'm a

goner one more time. And you seize me and whirl me about, dark
words I'm mortgaged to:
my owners, my darlings, my own.
To whom have I belonged, if not to you?

16

Small breeze, high
whispering oak-leaves.   And I'm
here, a thankful live one.
Tomorrow, new dues.
But tonight there is
nothing to prove; just wait, just
move in the night's warm body.
Body of edges.   Body of
stillness.   Body of breathing.

Looking back – what made me run? What pushed me
year by year by year
through all those loves and jobs and drafts and last-ditch causes?
It was hunger. Hunger. And, deeper than every
nerve-end purr in the pleasure machines of the *polis,* it was
unfilled hunger. Though for what, I can't tell.
Outside the museums, the names of the sacred no longer work.
They say too much, they say nothing at all and
though it seems strange to me,
I cannot find words to declare what my heart was hungering for.

For the old ones grew exotic.
Marduk, Loki, Vishnu –
amen of dispersal;
Manitou, Ishtar, Zeus –
rustle of silent goodbye.
They have become a rare, achieved, and
dangerous hole in the species, residual nothing,
the space a passing makes –
Yü-huang, Utnapishtim, Quetzalcoatl;
Persephone, Yahweh, God.

For we rose. And thought. And trashed our sacramental
birthright.
But I have lived 45 years, and never once
have I inched beyond the safety of lament …
But that's not what I *feel.* It's a playful itch,
a volt of desire, which
hankers towards what

God was a blasphemy of – never yet
have I danced full-tilt with my secret appetite:
                    to live in awe.

            To live, at last, in awe.
                    And I know, many reclaim that
        sanity at the margins, where our bodies still sense
                the tang of indigenous meaning. Returning to
                    granite, to cedar and loon – old
        amniotic siblings.
Or, catgut hosannas; held in that burnished ache of sound, how the
        soulmeat champs and respires!
                    Even graft and torture provoke it, the outraged
        sense of a justice we half belong to, half can't find.

                But now we live
        closer to zero noon, and what I know best
                    is the simple need.
            To flare in the wordless dimension. To hunch in my
                    other name, that doesn't have
I all over it.   Almost it hurts to relax.
            But in that arterial stammer, my back to words,
                    the yen just breathes.
            No storms of presence. My mind still yacks and fidgets.
But hunger hungers, and
                    sometimes I am permitted to mooch in the nearness.

That creatures are not enough.
Hawkmoth and tanager snag me; muskies re-
                    call me, though alien in weedkill; raccoons
        with their savvy instinctual poise haul me back to earth and,
wired in their unwitting circuits, bobtail and carapace all
                    species invade me,
    tangling my reified soul once more in the bone fraternity
            of things that are born and die –
    yet though I crave it,
                        kinship and diastole the
        creatures are not enough.

        And roots are not enough.   Such
bounty I came to! heart residence on earth, and I have loved
    a patch of ground too well: confess, confess at
                    dusk each summer long how a boy stood
            claimed by the hush of the Shield – the slow dark
        blotting the pines, and across the fretted
    lake the loons re-echoed, and the excellent chill of infinity
entered my blood to stay as I went on listening, went on
            listening.   I was practising my life among
    rocky companions, but the
            place is gone.

        People, I hear we are catastrophe.
    I hear we are strangers here.   For though we
            re-fashion earth in our image,

though in our hunger to nest we disnify the real,
I hear we have no home. No
home but hunger.

And precious, precious the dear ones – but also, that
dear ones are not enough. What man has been
lucky in love like me? raised in a warm, in a
principled sprawl of a family; gifted with luminous
friends, who make low-rent jokes and live their lives nobly;
and quickened by eros – hard in its seasons, but holy and
gracias, rare woman; and children who fasten my heart.
Yet what will endure in time? and whom do I own?
Was I not given such
peerless companions that I might learn to say, in love, *Not*
you, dear heart; nor you; nor you –
go by?

The text face in this book
is MINION, designed by Robert Slimbach.
The titling face is NOFRET, designed by Gudrun Zapf von Hesse.
Nightwatch was set into type by Susanne Gilbert
at The Typeworks, Vancouver.

¶ The Modern Canadian Poets Series presents the finest poetry of contemporary English Canada. Each volume is drawn from the work of a single writer, either at mid-career or after a lifetime's achievement. General editors for the series have been Dennis Lee, Russell Brown, Sam Solecki, and, as of 1993, Stan Dragland.

THE MODERN CANADIAN POETS SERIES
TITLES AVAILABLE

Acorn, Milton	*Dig Up My Heart*
Avison, Margaret	*Winter Sun / The Dumbfounding*
Bowering, George	*George Bowering Selected*
Bringhurst, Robert	*The Calling*
Coles, Don	*Landslides*
Dewdney, Christopher	*Predators of the Adoration*
Ford, R.A.D.	*Coming from Afar*
Kroetsch, Robert	*Completed Field Notes*
Layton, Irving	*A Wild Peculiar Joy*
Lee, Dennis	*Nightwatch*
LePan, Douglas	*Weathering It*
Nichol, bp	*An H in the Heart*
Rosenblatt, Joe	*Poetry Hotel*

OTHER COLLECTIONS OF SELECTED POEMS AVAILABLE
FROM MCCLELLAND & STEWART:

Birney, Earle	*Ghost in the Wheels*
Cohen, Leonard	*Stranger Music: Selected Poems and Songs*
Ondaatje, Michael	*The Cinnamon Peeler*
	There's a Trick with a Knife I'm Learning to Do
Purdy, Al	*The Collected Poems of Al Purdy*